THE CRUELEST JOURNEY

THE CRUELEST JOURNEY

600 MILES TO TIMBUKTU

KIRA SALAK

NATIONAL GEOGRAPHIC
WASHINGTON, D.C.

For my mother and her own journey, with love

Published by the National Geographic Society

Printed in the U.S.A.
Design by Melissa Farris, design production by Ted Tucker

Library of Congress Cataloging-in-Publication Data Available Upon Request

One of the world's largest nonprofit scientific and educational organizations, the National Geographic Society was founded in 1888 "for the increase and diffusion of geographic knowledge." Fulfilling this mission, the Society educates and inspires millions every day through its magazines, books, television programs, videos, maps and atlases, research grants, the National Geographic Bee, teacher workshops, and innovative classroom materials.

The Society is supported through membership dues, charitable gifts, and income from the sale of its educational products. This support is vital to National Geographic's mission to increase global understanding and promote con-servation of our planet through exploration, research, and education.

For more information, please call 1-800-NGS LINE (647-5463) or write to the following address:
National Geographic Society
1145 17th Street N.W.
Washington, D.C. 20036-4688 U.S.A.

Visit the Society's Web site at www.nationalgeographic.com.

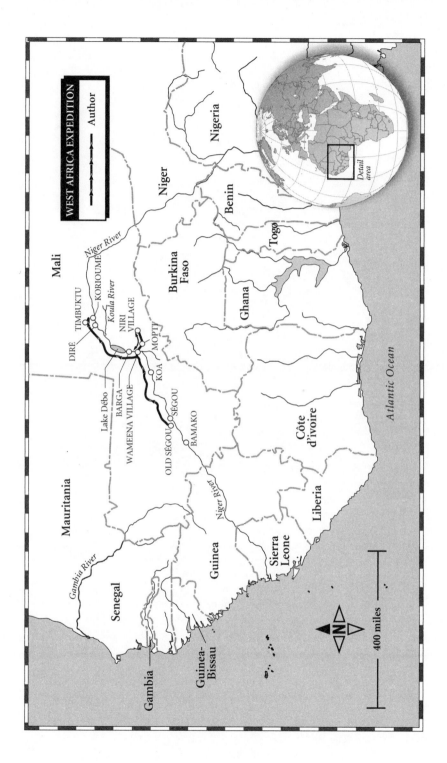

WEST AFRICA EXPEDITION

— Author

Mali

Niger River

KORIOUME

Koula River

TIMBUKTU

NIRI VILLAGE

DIRÉ

Lake Débo

BARGA

WAMEENA VILLAGE

MOPTI

KOA

SÉGOU

OLD SÉGOU

BAMAKO

Niger River

Mauritania

Gambia River

Senegal

Gambia

Guinea-Bissau

Guinea

Sierra Leone

Liberia

Côte d'Ivoire

Ghana

Burkina Faso

Togo

Benin

Niger

Nigeria

Atlantic Ocean

Detail area

N

400 miles

And I tell you, if you have the desire for knowledge and the power to give it physical expression, go out and explore…. Some will tell you that you are mad, and nearly all will say, "What is the use?" For we are a nation of shopkeepers, and no shopkeeper will look at research which does not promise him a financial return within a year. And so you will sledge nearly alone, but those with whom you sledge will not be shopkeepers: that is worth a great deal. If you march your Winter Journeys you will have your reward, so long as all you want is a penguin's egg.

—APSLEY CHERRY-GARRARD
The Worst Journey in the World

The winds roared, and the rains fell.
The poor white man, faint and weary, came and sat under our tree.
He has no mother to bring him milk; no wife to grind his corn.
Let us pity the white man; no mother has he.

—NATIVE BALLAD WRITTEN ABOUT MUNGO PARK
SÉGOU KORRO, 1796

PROLOGUE

Wide Afric, doth thy sun
Lighten, thy hills unfold a city as fair
As those which starred the night o' the elder world?
Or is the rumour of thy Timbuctoo
A dream as frail as those of ancient time?

—TENNYSON

I CAN'T IMAGINE TIMBUKTU HERE. I STAY IN ANOTHER OF THE WORLD'S cheap hotel rooms, this time in Mali, West Africa, in the capital city of Bamako. Cockroaches crouch behind the cracked porcelain toilet bowl; beetles climb the walls; mosquitoes hover over me, half-dazed. Unsavory couples check in to rooms next door, checking out a couple of hours later. But I'm fortunate because my room includes a shower, however basic, with a weary trickle of water. The electricity goes out at 9 a.m. sharp, turning off a rickety overhead fan, allowing the heat to filter through a pitted screen over the window and settle on my skin like a balm. I lie on a thin green cotton bedspread, wondering when it was last washed, trying to guess the source of the various stains on it. The frenetic sound of Bamako traffic invades through the wooden shutters that I always keep closed over the window. I hear a crashing sound from cars on the street—the usual, familiar crashing sound that I only seem to hear from such rooms—followed by yells in incensed Bambarra. Then, once again, the growls of passing motorbikes and the return of the dull, featureless mulling of crowds.

I roll onto my side, listening, studying, trying to memorize the poverty. The bloody smears of dead mosquitoes on the whitewashed wall before me. A floor that, if stepped on, leaves dust and strangers' hairs and fallen stucco from the ceiling clinging to the soles of my feet. A TV roaring from the room of the guy down the hall, whose job it is to clean these rooms, though of course he only makes the beds. The toilet smelling strongly of piss. The bed reeking of mildew and pungent sweat. The sink drip-dripping water with the certainty of a second hand.

Very little changes about these rooms except the languages I hear through the window, or the color of the bedspreads, or the wattage of the single overhead lightbulb. These are rooms that wake me in the middle of the night. Rooms that hold their darkness in gravid pause. Rooms that require sleeping pills because I so badly want the day back. They tell me when it's time to leave. They start all my journeys.

CHAPTER ONE

⤳

In the beginning, my journeys feel at best ludicrous, at worst insane. This one is no exception. The idea is to paddle nearly 600 miles on the Niger River in a kayak, alone, from the Malian town of Old Ségou to Timbuktu. And now, at the very hour when I have decided to leave, a thunderstorm bursts open the skies, sending down apocalyptic rain, washing away the very ground beneath my feet. It is the rainy season in Mali, for which there can be no comparison in the world. Lightning pierces trees, slices across houses. Thunder racks the skies and pounds the earth like mortar fire, and every living thing huddles in tenuous shelter, expecting the world to end. Which it doesn't. At least not this time. So that we all give a collective sigh to the salvation of the passing storm as it rumbles its way east, and I survey the river I'm to leave on this morning. Rain or no rain, today is the day for the journey to begin. And no one, not even the oldest in the village, can say for certain whether I'll get to the end.

"Let's do it," I say, leaving the shelter of an adobe hut. My guide from town, Modibo, points to the north, to further storms. He says he will pray for me. It's the best he can do. To his knowledge, no man has ever completed such a trip, though a few have tried. And certainly no woman has done such a thing. This morning he took me aside and told me he thinks I'm crazy, which I understood as concern and thanked him. He told me that the people of Old Ségou think I'm crazy too, and that only uncanny good luck will keep me safe.

Still, when a person tells me I can't do something, I'll want to do it all the more. It may be a failing of mine. I carry my inflatable kayak through the narrow passageways of Old Ségou, past the small adobe huts melting in the rains, past the huddling goats and smoke of cooking fires, people peering out at me from the dark entranceways. It is a labyrinth of ancient homes, built and rebuilt after each storm, plastered with the very earth people walk upon. Old Ségou must look much the same as it did in Scottish explorer Mungo Park's time when, exactly 206 years ago to the day, he left on the first of his two river journeys down the Niger to Timbuktu, the first such attempt by a Westerner. It is no coincidence that I've planned to leave on the same day and from the same spot. Park is my benefactor of sorts, my guarantee. If he could travel down the Niger, then so can I. And it is all the guarantee I have for this trip—that an obsessed 19th-century adventurer did what I would like to do. Of course Park also died on this river, but I've so far managed to overlook that.

I gaze at the Niger through the adobe passageways, staring at waters that began in the mountainous rain forests of Guinea and traveled all this way to central Mali—waters that will journey northeast with me to Timbuktu before cutting a great circular swath through the Sahara and retreating south, through Niger, on to Nigeria, passing circuitously through mangrove swamps and jungle, resting at last in the Atlantic in the Bight of Benin. But the Niger is more than a river; it is a kind of faith. Bent and plied by Saharan sands, it perseveres more than 2,600 miles from beginning to end through one of the hottest, most desolate regions of the world. And when the rains come each year, it finds new strength of purpose, surging through the sunbaked lands, giving people the boons of crops and livestock and fish, taking nothing, asking nothing. It humbles all who see it.

If I were to try to explain why I'm here, why I chose Mali and the Niger for this journey—now that is a different matter. I can already feel the resistance in my gut, the familiar clutch of fear. I used to avoid stripping myself down in search of motivation, scared of what I might uncover, scared of anything that might suggest a taint of the pathological. And would it be enough to say that I admire Park's own trip on the river and want to try a similar challenge? That answer carries a whiff of the disingenuous; it sounds too easy to me. Human motivation, itself, is a complicated thing. If only it was simple enough to say, "Here is the Niger, and I want to paddle it." But I'm not that kind of traveler, and this isn't that kind of trip. If a journey doesn't have something to teach you about yourself, then what kind of journey is it? There is one thing I'm already certain of: Though we may think we choose our journeys, they choose us.

Hobbled donkeys cower under a new onslaught of rain, ears back, necks craned. Little naked children dare each other to touch me, and I make it easy for them, stopping and holding out my arm. They stroke my white skin as if it were velvet, using only the pads of their fingers, then stare at their hands to check for wet paint.

Thunder again. More rain falls. I stop on the shore, near a centuries-old kapok tree under which I imagine Park once took shade. I open my bag, spread out my little red kayak, and start to pump it up. I'm doing this trip under the sponsorship of *National Geographic Adventure*, which hopes to run a magazine story about it. This means that they need photos, lots of photos, and so a French photographer named Rémi

Bénali feverishly snaps pictures of me. I don't know what I hate more—river storms or photo shoots. I value the privacy and integrity of my trips, and I don't want my journey turning into a circus. The magazine presented the best compromise it could: Rémi, renting a motor-driven pirogue, was given instructions to find me on the river every few days to do his thing.

My kayak is nearly inflated. A couple of women nearby, with colorful cloth wraps called *pagnes* tied tightly about their breasts, gaze at me cryptically, as if to ask: *Who are you and what do you think you're doing?* The Niger churns and slaps the shore, in a surly mood. I don't pretend to know what I'm doing. Just one thing at a time now, kayak inflated, kayak loaded with my gear. Paddles fitted together and ready. Modibo is standing on the shore, watching me.

"I'll pray for you," he reminds me.

I balance my gear, adjust the straps, get in. And, finally, irrevocably, I paddle away.

When Mungo Park left on his second trip, he never admitted that he was scared. It is what fascinates me about his writing—his insistence on maintaining an illusion that all was well, even as he began a journey that he knew from previous experience could only beget tragedy. Hostile peoples, unknown rapids, malarial fevers. Hippos and crocodiles. The giant Lake Debo to cross, like being set adrift on an inland sea, no sight of land, no way of knowing where the river starts again. Forty of his forty-four men dead from sickness, Park himself afflicted with dysentery when he left on this trip. And it can boggle the mind, what drives some people to risk their lives for the mute promises of success. It boggles my mind, at least, as I am caught up in the same affliction. Already, I fear the irrationality of my journey, the relentless stubbornness that drives me on.

The storm erupts into a new overture. Torrential rains. Waves higher than my kayak, trying to capsize me. But my boat is self-bailing and I stay afloat. The wind drives the current in reverse, tearing and ripping at the shores, sending spray into my face. I paddle madly, crashing and driving forward. I travel inch by inch, or so it seems, arm muscles smarting and rebelling against this journey. I crawl past New Ségou, fighting the Niger for more distance. Large river steamers rest in jumbled rows before cement docks, the town itself looking dark and deserted in the downpour. No one is out in their boats. The people know something I don't: that the river dictates all travel.

A popping feeling now and a screech of pain. My right arm lurches from a ripped muscle. But this is no time and place for such an injury, and I won't tolerate it, stuck as I am in a storm. I try to get used to the pulses of pain as I fight the river. There is only one direction to go: forward. Stopping has become anathema.

~

I WONDER WHAT WE LOOK FOR WHEN WE EMBARK ON THESE KINDS OF trips. There is the pat answer that you tell the people you don't know: that you're interested in seeing a place, learning about its people. But then the trip begins and the hardship comes, and hardship is more honest: it tells us that we don't have enough patience yet, nor humility, nor gratitude. And we thought that we did. Hardship brings us closer to truth, and thus is more difficult to bear, but from it alone comes compassion. And so I've told the world that it can do what it wants with me during this trip if only, by the end, I have learned something more. A bargain, then. The journey, my teacher.

And where is the river of just this morning, with its whitecaps that would have liked to drown me, with its current flowing backward against the wind? Gone to this: a river of smoothest glass, a placidity unbroken by wave or eddy, with islands of lush greenery awaiting me like distant Xanadus. The Niger is like a mercurial god, meting out punishment and benediction on a whim. And perhaps the god of the river sleeps now, returning matters to the mortals who ply its waters? The Bozo and Somono fishermen in their pointy canoes. The long passenger pirogues, overloaded with people and merchandise, rumbling past, leaving diesel fumes in their wake. And now, inexplicably, the white woman in a little red boat, paddling through waters that flawlessly mirror the cumulus clouds above. We all belong here, in our way. It is as if I've entered a very lucid dream, continually surprised to find myself here on this river—I've become a hapless actor in a mysterious play, not yet knowing what my part is, left to gape at the wonder of what I have set in motion. Somehow: I'm in a kayak, on the Niger River, paddling very slowly but very surely to Timbuktu.

I pass tiny villages of adobe huts on the shores, some large and full of busy work: women washing clothes and dishes in the river, children chasing after goats, men repairing fishing nets. In other villages, some smaller and less permanent-looking with huts made from mud and thatch, men lounge beneath trees and swat flies and talk. The women pound millet with wooden pestles the size of a small child. I get used to the certainty of their up and down movements, the *thump* of the pestle in the stone mortar, again and again, like a drumbeat. It is the music of rural Mali, as are the fervent calls of the children when I pass, and the great bellowing of donkeys that could surely be heard on the other side of the world. Each village has its own mud mosque sending squat minarets to the heavens. There is nothing glamorous about the architecture—no sharp angles or filigree or carvings—but it is this very unprepossessing quality that makes the mosques special. Like mud castles of childhood fancy, they seem built from some latent creative energy, spiky sticks topping the minarets, ostrich eggs beacon-like on the highest points, with small portholes carved from the mud sides and staring out enigmatically at the traveler. The impulse is to stop and try to peek inside, to get a look at the dark interior, the primordial secrets within.

But I only pass by. The mosques in these parts probably wouldn't be open to me. Before my trip began, I asked to see one in a riverside village, and the imam (head of the mosque) solemnly shook his head. A reason was translated to me: I'm an "infidel," a sinner. I would not even be allowed to climb the outside stairs. He also called me a Christian, and though he was incorrect (I practice Buddhism), I felt a tweaking in my stomach that was part anger, part sorrow: I had been summed up and dismissed in a matter of seconds. But surely it's human nature to overlook similarities for differences, people fortifying imaginary walls between themselves more insurmountable than any made from stone.

The late afternoon sun settles complacently over the hills to the west. Paddling becomes a sort of meditation now, a gentle trespassing over a river that slumbers. The Niger gives me its beauty almost in apology for the violence of the earlier storms, treating me to smooth silver waters that ripple in the sunlight. The current—if there is one—barely moves. Park described the same grandeur of the Niger during his second journey, in an uncharacteristically sentimental passage that provided a welcome respite from accounts of dying soldiers and baggage stolen by natives: "We travelled very pleasantly all day; in fact nothing can be more beautiful than the views of this immense river; sometimes as smooth as a mirror, at other times ruffled with a gentle breeze, but at all times sweeping us along at the rate of six or seven miles per hour."

I barely travel at one mile an hour, the river preferring—as I do—to loiter in the sun. I lean down in my seat and hang my feet over the sides of the kayak. I eat turkey jerky and wrap up my injured arm, part of which has swollen to the size of a grapefruit. I'm not worried about the injury anymore. I'm not worried about anything. I know this feeling won't last, but for now I wrap myself in it, feeling the rare peace. To reach a place of not worrying is a greater freedom than anything I could hope to find on one of these trips. It is my true Undiscovered Country.

The Somono fishermen, casting out their nets, puzzle over me as I float by.

"*Ça va, madame?*" they yell.

Each fisherman carries a young son perched in the back of his pointed canoe to do the paddling. The boys stare at me, transfixed; they have never seen such a thing. A white woman. Alone. In a red, inflatable boat. Using a two-sided paddle.

I'm an even greater novelty because Malian women don't paddle here, not ever. It is a man's job. So there is no good explanation for me, and the people want to understand. They want to see if I'm strong enough for it, or if I even know how to use a paddle. They want to determine how sturdy my boat is. They gather on the shore in front of their villages to watch me pass, the kids screaming and jumping in excitement, the women with hands to foreheads to shield the sun as they stare, men yelling out questions in Bambarra which by now I know to mean: "Where did you come from? Are you alone? Where's your husband?" And of course they will always ask: "Where are you going?"

"Timbuktu!" I yell out to the last question. Which sounds preposterous to them, because everyone knows that Timbuktu is weeks away, and requires paddling across Lake Debo somehow, and through rapids and storms. And I am a woman, after all, which must make everything worse.

"*Tombouctou!?!*" they always repeat, just to be sure.

"*Awo*," I say in the Bambarra I've learned. "Yes."

Head shakes. Shared grins. We wave goodbye, and the whole ritual begins at the next village. And at the next, and the next after that, kids running beside me along the shore, singing out their frantic choruses of "*Ça va! Ça va!*" I might be the pope, or someone close. But in between is the peace and silence of the wide river, the sun on me, a breeze licking my toes when I lie back to rest, the current as negligible as a faint breath.

I think often about Mungo Park's journeys to this country, which were anything but easy for him. But he was a tough young Scot and had an impressive fortitude to endure with hardship. Park was only 23 years old when he left on his first journey to West Africa in search of the Niger River and Timbuktu. He was not without striking, fascinating contradictions in character. He was by any standards a devoutly spiritual man, convinced that the vagaries of life have their place in God's scheme of things. He would write:

> "The melancholy, who complain of the shortness of human life, and the voluptuous, who think the present only their own, strive to fill up every moment with sensual enjoyment; but the man whose soul has been enlightened by his Creator, and enabled, though dimly, to discern the wonders of salvation, will look upon the joys and afflictions of this life as equally the tokens of Divine love. He will walk through the world as one travelling to a better country, looking forward with wonder to the author and finisher of his faith."

But he was also a pragmatist who could be lured by the trappings of future fame, confiding in his brother that he would "acquire a name greater than any ever did." Was this merely explorer's hubris? Or was it also the source of Park's extraordinary ability to endure difficulty and danger?

During any kind of journey, when virtually nothing is within one's control, when nothing can be sufficiently anticipated or prepared for, a great deal of hubris is necessary. I must tell myself now, for example, that I can get to Timbuktu. I must say it as if it were already so, assuring myself that I'm fit enough to do it, that I can condition my mind to survive on little food, in great heat, in unpleasant conditions, with no companions to assist me. Much can be learned from Park's heady pre-trip declaration that he would "acquire a name greater than any ever did." Self-confidence for any difficult or risky endeavor relies largely on the power of imagination, on a person's ability to see the end before the end has come, to see oneself exactly where one would like to be.

And you can never know what will happen. Before my departure to Mali, I told my parents what to do with my things if I didn't come back. It wasn't melodrama; I was quite serious. They're used to hearing that from me, I suppose, as I've said it before other trips, but they still don't get used to my insistence on going anyway. They don't *understand* that insistence, as they expend a lot of energy in not disturbing the routine of their lives with anything new that lacks a guarantee. And I certainly don't criticize them for that; it is who they are. But I've always found myself unsettled by predictability, routine, comfort; I'm lulled by these things, and bored by them, and then my mind turns in on itself and obsesses about utter minutiae. I need doses of the new before me, the strange, the completely unfamiliar, in order to feel truly alive. This probably started early for me. As a child, I never felt an intrinsic sense of belonging anywhere; I've always been fascinated by those who feel rooted to a place, for whom wanderlust becomes a pathology of the soul. All I know is that my trips allow me to unearth parts of myself that I've long since buried as dead, showing me who I can be. They are, in many respects, processes of rebirth.

I stop paddling to watch a fragile white butterfly beat its way across the Niger, across a river that is easily a mile wide. Where does this tiny creature get its energy to pump those wings? It flutters and dives above my kayak, already halfway across the river, another half mile to go. All around it is the sure death of these silver waters, and no wind to help it along. By what will did it make this crossing? And to what? The greenery on both sides of the Niger looks the same. I hold up the respite of my paddle blade, but it swirls away toward the sun and continues on.

I think of Park, who earned a place in history's annals as one of the most intrepid and craziest explorers that ever lived. He embarked into an unmapped part of the world that existed in the minds of Europeans solely as speculation, myth, or hearsay. It was a country known for its hostile peoples and notoriously fatal diseases; if he got into trouble, there would be absolutely no one to help him. Park's unwavering ambition has always fascinated me. I'm hoping that, by duplicating his journey as best I can, I will come to know what drove him alone into West Africa's interior. Some historians have suggested that he had a death wish or was mad. Others claim he was interested in money or fame. But I suspect that Park possessed an uncanny and insatiable curiosity for the unknown, which was fed all the more by this spectacular country: the verdant shores, the somnolent waters, a sun that dazzles the river with light. Park, a product of Scotland's dreary moors, must have found Mali a blithe country.

In December 1795 he began his first journey to the Niger River from the British river port of Pisania, in modern-day Gambia, in the company of an African man hired as a translator and a Mandingo slave boy, who, owned by a local British doctor, had been ordered to accompany him (the doctor had promised the boy his freedom if he and Park ever successfully returned—though the doctor had his doubts). "I believe," Park wrote, "[that the doctor and his acquaintances] secretly thought they should never see me afterwards." Indeed, the Association for the Promotion of the Discovery of Africa—Park's London sponsors—had already sent three explorers on identical quests to try to reach the Niger and Timbuktu, one turning back and two dying in the attempt. Park was their latest hopeful, but the meager 200-pound advance they gave him for his transportation costs and supplies suggests they had little faith in him. None of this seemed to faze Park, though, and he headed east along the Gambia River without any knowledge of or experience in Africa, riding across what is now Senegal into Mali, with only his two companions, provisions for a couple of days, tobacco and beads for village bartering, a compass, a sextant, muskets, spare clothing, and all the blind, reckless will in the world.

I feel not unlike Park, with my own meager remuneration promised me from the National Geographic Society if I should succeed—*if*— and a single backpack in my kayak holding everything that I hope will suffice for my trip. I stop paddling to pump Niger River water into my bottles, dropping the filtration pump's tube into a river rife with raw sewage, marveling at the clear water coming out the other end. Just to be on the safe side, I plop in a couple of iodine tablets. In such a way, I suppose it could be said that my needs are all met—for at least as long as my turkey jerky holds out.

When Park traveled, local kings kept begging him to turn back, warning that the interior tribes would have never seen a white man or his European goodies. Park, of course, continued. He came across people who had never seen the likes of him but were too afraid to approach. "Two Negro horsemen," Park wrote in his narrative, "armed with muskets, came galloping from among the bushes: on seeing them I made a full stop; the horsemen did the same, and all three of us seemed equally surprised and confounded at this interview. As I approached them their fears increased, and one of them, after casting upon me a look of horror, rode off at full speed; the other, in a panic of fear, put his hand over his eyes, and continued muttering prayers until his horse, seemingly without the rider's knowledge, conveyed him slowly after his companion." Park's luck would run out when the Moors, a North African Arab people living in parts of Mali, heard about the strange white man. They caught up with Park and robbed him of everything but the clothes on his back, his hat, and his compass (thought to be an evil talisman), keeping him prisoner in the deserts of what is now Mauritania. It would become the darkest time of Park's first journey.

I found this part of his narrative the most poignant. He doesn't hide his distress, and his trademark equanimity fails him, revealing glimpses of a traumatizing ordeal. Many male adventurers of his time chose to hide such candor, opting instead for bravado or tedious ethnographical digressions. But Park did not want his own suffering or others' to pass without witness. When the Mandingo boy with Park was seized into slavery by the Moors, Park became hopelessly distraught. He had come to care about him like a son. "I [shook] hands with this unfortunate boy," Park wrote, "and blended my tears with his, assuring him, however, that I would do my utmost to redeem him." The boy would never be seen again. Park was left alone among strangers, kept prisoner in a tent in the Sahara during the most scorching months of the year, enduring dawn to dusk taunts from crowds of Moors and a humiliating lack of privacy. At one point a wild hog was tied beside him:

> This animal had certainly been placed there by ...
> order [of Ali, Park's captor] out of derision to a

Christian; and I found it a very disagreeable inmate,
as it drew together a number of boys, who amused
themselves by beating it with sticks, until they had
so irritated the hog that it ran and bit at every person within its reach.... With the returning day com-
menced the same round of insult and irritation:
the boys assembled to beat the hog, and the men and
women to plague the Christian.

But even Park's grim trip had its moments of comic relief. Moorish
women were Park's most frequent visitors. He tells us, "they asked [me]
a thousand questions; inspected every part of my apparel, searched
my pockets, and obliged me to unbutton my waistcoat and display
the whiteness of my skin: they even counted my toes and fingers, as
if they doubted whether I was in truth a human being ... and in this
manner I was employed, dressing and undressing, buttoning and
unbuttoning, from noon to night." It turns out that the women were
interested in inspecting one part of his anatomy in particular. Park tells
of this experience with his usual air of propriety, but it was nonetheless a passage that shocked and amused his early 19th-century
readership: "A party of [women] came into my hut, and gave me
plainly to understand that the object of their visit was to ascertain,
by actual inspection, whether the rite of circumcision extended to the
Nazarenes (Christians), as well as to the followers of Mahomet."
Park handled the situation deftly, declaring that only the youngest and
most beautiful of the women would be allowed an exclusive view. Still,
Park tells us that the chosen woman "did not avail herself of the
privilege of inspection."

The humor is short-lived after that. At one point during Park's captivity, he found himself gravely ill. He entreated the Moors to leave him

alone to recuperate, discovering that he had "solicited in vain: my distress was a matter of sport to them, and they endeavored to heighten it, by every means in their power. This studied and degrading insolence, to which I was constantly exposed, was one of the bitterest ingredients in the cup of captivity; and often made life itself a burden to me." The days turned into months. During a wedding party, an old woman threw a bowl of bridal urine in his face. Park was subsequently threatened with death, with the amputation of his right hand, with having his eyes poked out. But, somehow, the intrepid Scotsman kept his cool, acquiescing to nearly every request, never losing his temper, never getting self-righteous—behavior that certainly saved his life. Park wrote, "I readily complied with every command, and patiently bore every insult; but never did any period of my life pass away so heavily: from sunrise to sunset, was I obliged to suffer, with an unruffled countenance."

Park's trials among the Moors would give him unremitting nightmares for years, long after he launched a brave escape from them in the middle of the night and made his way back to England to write his narrative. I try to imagine Park during this darkest time, spending lonely, fitful nights in confinement in the desert, wondering if the next day would see him losing his eyes, having a hand cut off, being killed in some horrible way. What thoughts about his journey then? What doubts? "But the man whose soul has been enlightened by his Creator," Park wrote, "will look upon the joys and afflictions of this life as equally the tokens of Divine love." Did Park have the wherewithal to take a step back from his suffering long enough to see it all as part of some grand scheme, as a token of "Divine love" meant to teach him about the nature of existence? This is for me one of the hardest notions to fathom: that life's most tragic events, its greatest sufferings, unfold with some kind of arcane purpose and design. It shoots anger and sadness through my heart. It troubles my mind with questions.

We do know that Park not only survived his treatment, seizing an opportunity to escape, but that he *continued* on his quest to find the Niger. He led a skeletal horse through the sandy plains of central Mali, begging for food at villages, escaping from bandits and ill-wishers, nearly dying of thirst. Miraculously, he reached the Niger. He would later be credited with having been, in 1797, the first Western explorer to discover the river, which helped to make his ensuing narrative, *Travels in the Interior Districts of Africa*, a bestseller. Park took care to describe the moment: "I saw with infinite pleasure the great object of my mission: the long sought for, majestic Niger, glittering to the morning sun, as broad as the Thames at Westminster, and flowing slowly to the *eastward*. I hastened to the brink, and, having drank of the water, lifted up my fervent thanks in prayer, to the Great Ruler of all things, for having thus far crowned my endeavors with success." But Park's enthusiasm for his discovery miffed the local peoples, who of course had known about the Niger for millennia and had their own name for it—the Joliba, or Great Water. The sight of a bedraggled white man staring at its shores, composing lofty paeans to its name, puzzled them. Park would write of a Bambarra man's reaction: "When he was told that I had come from a great distance, and through many dangers, to behold the Joliba river, [he] naturally inquired if there were no rivers in my own country, and whether one river was not like another." Fitting.

As I travel the river, I wonder if the Bozo or Somono fishermen have the same questions about me. What brings me here? Don't I have rivers closer to home? Why come to their Niger? Most people in these parts will have never been any farther than Bamako, if they have been anywhere at all. For them, traveling is undertaken for some sort of pragmatic purpose. They might pole their canoes along to attend a village market, or they might make a longer journey to town to buy some hard-to-find supplies. But to travel the river for the sake of traveling? Now that idea must be strange, indeed. And how would I explain it? Certainly, my presence here is the result of growing up in a wealthy society that affords many of its people the chance for such specialized pursuits. I know I come to Mali out of this position, and this fact has always embarrassed me about traveling in developing countries, but has also incited me to try to understand the forces that have denied such a standard of life to the majority of the people I encounter.

The sun begins to fall behind some distant hills. I look out at Park's "majestic Niger," the soft waters catching the orange of the departing sun. I wonder if such a sight would have been enough reward for the travails he had suffered: loss of all his possessions, brutal confinement by the Moors, half-starved wanderings in the Malian desert. I recall a conversation Park had with a local king: "I repeated what I had before told [the king] concerning the ... reasons for passing through his country. He seemed, however, but half-satis-fied. The notion of traveling for curiosity was quite new to him. He thought it impossible, he said, that any man in his senses would undertake so dangerous a journey merely to look at the country and its inhabitants." Before the discovery and use of quinine to cure malaria, travel to West Africa was a virtual death sentence for Europeans, akin to being sent to the Russian Front. Colonial powers used only their most insubordinate and expendable soldiers, many of them petty thieves and criminals, to man the forts and oversee oper-ations on the coast. It wasn't uncommon for expeditions to lose half their men to fever and dysentery, if the natives didn't get them first. So Mungo Park's ambitious plan of heading up the Gambia River, cross-ing what is now Senegal into Mali, then heading by boat up the Niger River to Timbuktu, hadn't a modern-day equivalent. It was beyond gutsy—it was borderline suicidal.

Park's troubles didn't end upon his discovery of the river. Mansong, the king of an area then known as Bambarra, tried to get the destitute white man off his hands by giving him money and encouraging him to get out of town and go back to his own people. Park didn't take the hint. He instead began the first of his two river journeys on the Niger from the site of present-day Old Ségou or Ségou Korro—my own starting point. But, surprisingly for Park, he gave up this first venture, providing this explanation:

> Worn down by sickness, exhausted by hunger and fatigue; half naked, and without any article of value, by which I might procure provisions, clothes or lodging; I began to reflect seriously on my situation. I was now convinced, by painful experience, that the obstacles to my further progress were insurmountable.... I had but little hopes of subsisting by charity, in a country where the Moors have such influence. But above all, I perceived that I was advancing, more and more, within the power of those merciless fanatics; and ... I was apprehensive that I should sacrifice my life to no purpose; for my discoveries would perish with me.

Park made an extraordinary decision for a man so stubbornly possessed by his journey—he decided to make the long trip back home. Still, this return was just as fraught with uncertainty as a trip on the Niger would have been. But he had no choice. "Whichever way I turned," he wrote, "nothing appeared but danger and difficulty. I saw myself in the midst of a vast wilderness, in the depth of the rainy season; naked and alone; surrounded by savage animals, and men still more savage. I was five hundred miles from the nearest European settlement."

His retreat had barely begun when he was robbed and assaulted by bandits, who stripped him naked and left him to die in the desert. And here is the Mungo Park that I seek in my own journey, the man who, during this most desperate of times when his strength and will all but left him, noticed the beauty of some moss nearby, which he studied with infinite patience and admiration. "Can that Being," Park waxed, "who planted, watered, and brought to perfection, in this obscure part of the world, a thing which appears of so small importance, look with unconcern upon the situation and sufferings of creatures formed after his own image?—surely not! Reflections like these would not allow me to despair. I started up, and disregarding both hunger and fatigue, travelled forwards."

I can't imagine Park's difficulties. I have only an arm that is swelled and tender to move, each pull of the paddle causing jolts of pain. Such an injury would have never slowed down Park, let alone stopped him. Still, I wish this had occurred a week or two into my trip, not on the first day. Who knows if it will get better—or worse? I rewrap it with an Ace bandage and try to forget about it. Timbuktu or bust.

I find inspiration in the fact that Park weathered his trials, making it back to the coast and safely to England, where he became an instant celebrity with the publication of his book. Still, nine years later, he would return to West Africa, to the very country that had nearly killed him. Some historians believe he did it for the money. For all his success, Park never became rich, and his life as a country doctor in Scotland could barely make ends meet. But money troubles were only half the story. Park's venturesome spirit—like the proverbial genie let loose from the bottle—could no longer be contained. Scotland hardly compared to the fantastic world that had thrown open its doors to him. "I would rather brave Africa and all its horrors," Park confided to his friend Sir Walter Scott, "than wear out my life in long and toilsome rides over cold and lonely heaths and gloomy hills, assailed by the wintry tempest, for which the remuneration was hardly enough to keep body and soul together." Park knew that he possessed a rare ability to survive the worst kinds of adversity in the loneliest quarters of the world—a talent greatly in demand during the British Empire's heyday of colonial acquisition. He saw for himself an opportunity to better his prospects.

Park began petitioning the government for opportunities to lead expeditions abroad, in such places as the untamed lands of New South Wales (now southeastern Australia). He made visits to London with his requests, writing letters to his wife back in Scotland that were full of love and hope for financial security: "My lovely Ailie, you are constantly in my thoughts. I am tired of this place, but cannot lose the present opportunity of doing something for our advantage." His petitions would fail until the British government became interested in Africa again and offered Park an impressive commission: go back to West Africa, to the Niger, reach Timbuktu, and then figure out where the river terminates. This time Park would be lavishly outfitted, and he'd be accompanied by 44 British soldiers, to be chosen from those posted in forts by the Gambia River. For Park, this venture would not only yield a large financial boon if successful but would also mean an extraordinary achievement on behalf of God, King, and Country. Park readily agreed.

I approach a family traveling in a long dugout canoe—daughter, mother, grandmother, with the young sons and father doing all the paddling. We glide past each other, everyone looking at me with wonder, their hesitant smiles bursting into grins and laughter when I greet them in Bambarra: "*Iniché, somo-go?*" Hello, how is your family?

"*Toro-té, aniché,*" they respond. Fine, thank you.

I took pains to learn some of the basic words and phrases of the languages I would encounter along the next 600 miles of the river. Greetings, of course, but also very practical terms: "Is it close?" "Far?" "Here?" "Over there?" "Where am I?" and "I don't understand." I also learned words for items or animals I might have to buy or eat or, God forbid, avoid: fish, rice, hippo, crocodile. And, of course, I made sure I could say, "I'm going to Timbuktu!" (Colorfully, in the Songhai language: *Ye koi Tomboctoo!*)

Park must have made similar preparations for his return trip to the Niger in search of Timbuktu and the termination of the river. Presumably, he must have also pondered his odds of succeeding, deciding they were in his favor. After all, though alone and wretched on his first journey, he still managed to discover the Niger, and so what would 44 armed soldiers and a king's wealthy sponsorship do for him? The proposed second trip must have seemed laughably *easy* by comparison to his first journey. Park declared in a proposal to a government minister that his expedition would lead to "the extension of British commerce and the enlargement of our geographical knowledge." He was rewarded with a captain's commission, a generous subsidy of 5,000 pounds, and all the supplies and pack animals he needed for the journey.

His goals were explicitly outlined to him: he was to travel on the Niger River, visit Timbuktu and ascertain the wealth of the city and its environs, take note of the location of natural resources and prospective trade opportunities, determine the feasibility of European settlement, and find where the Niger terminates. It was this last directive that had been the subject of debate for centuries in Europe: Where did the Niger end? Though Europeans had long known about the river, no one had much information about it. Some believed it joined the

Nile. Others were convinced from faulty Greek accounts that it ended in a great inland sea. Still others believed it curved down and merged with the Congo River or actually passed *beneath* the Sahara, emptying into the Mediterranean. But regardless, everyone knew that with the secret of its course lay a means of opening up the African continent to commerce, and in particular a lucrative trade in gold. Discovering the route of the Niger and its mystical Timbuktu could make men rich, and could build empires.

And so Park went back for a second helping of the country that had nearly killed him. He left behind a wife and three children, a medical practice, and a fame that might have sustained his ego if not his pocketbook. Park reached the Gambian coast on 28 March 1805, political red tape and assorted other difficulties delaying his departure for the interior; it wasn't until the malarial rainy season that Park was prepared to go, and he vowed to begin regardless of the weather (any further delays might have inflamed his sponsors). In his predeparture letters, he maintained a cheerful attitude, making no reference to the tropical storms and their accompanying illnesses that would soon kill his men by the handful. No mention, either, that his soldiers were some of the poorest examples of military manpower in the British Empire, most of them drunkards, deserters, or navy convicts who were pardoned in exchange for accompanying Park on his crazy adventure. Ominously, Park had been unable to bribe or cajole any native recruits into joining him in his venture, a fact that he admitted to one of his superiors back in England: "No inducement," Park wrote, "could prevail on a single Negro to accompany me." But Park didn't openly despair. Surely he understood that any doubts on his part might be seen as a sign of unacceptable weakness. He had to uphold his reputation as one of Europe's greatest adventurers.

As Park headed toward the Niger, his journey barely under way, the first of a long series of mishaps and misfortunes befell him. Soldiers became sick with dysentery, giardia, malaria, yellow fever, and died one after the next. Severe storms further demoralized the remaining men. Natives incessantly robbed the sickly, undefended convoy, stealing animals and cargo. Rivers swelled with rain, men drowning in the attempt to cross. Hostile village chiefs extorted money. Wild animals—lions, crocodiles, hyenas—attacked the stragglers. Overburdened horses and donkeys died or refused to move. Even killer bees tormented the expedition. It was, in short, an utter disaster.

As I paddle along, night approaches, bringing with it concerns of where I can safely stop and sleep. I scan the banks of the river, not yet ready to break my solitude by pulling into a village for the evening. I can't say how I might be received by the local people, though the fishermen I've encountered have been friendly. One of the most frequently recurring themes in Park's narrative was a similar wariness about how he might be greeted at each new village. As he quickly discovered: you just have to take your chances.

Luck wasn't on Park's side when he made it to the Niger for the second time, 40 of his original 44 soldiers dead, all of his pack animals killed or stolen. It wasn't long before his closest companion on the expedition, a brother-in-law from Scotland, died. A distraught Park recorded the death in his journal, and it is one of the few times he so openly expresses his feelings of despair. Otherwise, he keeps up a masquerade of denial, insisting that he hadn't been affected by "the smallest gloom" until then. The events described in his journals tell a different story. In nearly every entry, there is only catastrophe. Dying soldiers being left behind. Park constantly backtracking in search of lost donkeys or sickly men. Natives robbing the hapless convoy at every opportunity, becoming bolder and bolder as the men suffered increasing illness. One finds it hard to believe that not "the smallest gloom" ever overshadowed poor Mungo Park and his operation.

But Park was determined to plug on—perhaps because, in addition to an enormous, irrational aversion to failure, he had also caught the Timbuktu fever of those times, calling the fabled city "the great object of my search." Having gone that far, he would rather die than give up his quest. With all his carpenters dead, he faced the daunting task of constructing a boat to sail on the Niger. At the same time, he was battling severe dysentery. Becoming gravely ill and fearing the failure of his mission, he did something well in tune with his remarkable fortitude—he poisoned his system to the point of near-death. "As I found that my strength was failing fast," Park wrote in his journal, "I resolved to change myself with mercury. I accordingly took calomel till it affected my mouth to such a degree that I could not speak or sleep for six days. The salivation put an immediate stop to the dysentery." One might wonder why he decided to continue with the journey, given all that had happened to him by this time. Historians speculate that Park had become so deranged by sickness that he couldn't think rationally anymore.

Park managed to piece together a couple of rotten canoes, outfitting his "H.M.S. *Joliba*" with rawhide shields to protect him from hostile tribes downriver. He wrote some final letters—to his wife and his sponsor, Lord Camden. To the latter, he maintained a sense of optimism that was nothing short of extraordinary, given the circumstances: "I am afraid your lordship will be apt to consider matters as in a very hopeless state, but I assure you I am far from desponding.... I shall set sail to the east with the fixed resolution to discover the termination of the Niger or perish in the attempt." And thus, he left the town of Sansanding, never to be seen again.

Of the river journey itself, none of Park's written accounts were recovered, so we can know nothing definitively. There are only the verbal recollections given by a guide and translator Park had hired. This man, Amadi Fatouma, described a journey plagued by tragedy: Park refusing to stop or leave his boat; local tribes chasing him in canoes and attacking him. If Fatouma is to be believed, Park had to shoot his way down the Niger. Apparently, Park spurned local kings, who demanded duties from him to pass through their kingdoms, armed men preventing him from landing at the port of Timbuktu. Though there are accounts other than Fatouma's that tell of Park's entering the golden city, we do know for certain that he never made it to the river's termination in the Atlantic Ocean. He drowned or was killed in the rapids of Bussa (in Nigeria), with the truth of where he stopped and what he saw dying with him. Thus began the legend of Mungo Park, the iron-willed adventurer extraordinaire, rumored to be the first white man ever to reach Timbuktu. At the very least, he was the first to have reached its port.

I float along in my kayak, night settling resolutely upon the river. I pull over, deciding to camp behind some reeds. The Niger's dark waters turn northeast, toward Timbuktu, a city as distant and unimaginable to me now as it must have been to Park, who had only the descriptions in a popular book to go on. Written in 1526 by slave-turned-scholar Leo Africanus, *History and Description of Africa and the Notable Things Contained Therein* described the city as a veritable El Dorado, a place of higher learning where palaces were steeped in gold. By all estimates, Africanus was not far off the mark. At the time he visited Timbuktu, it remained the height of wealth and haute couture, the pearl of West Africa's great Songhai Empire, home to universities, extensive libraries, Africa's largest and grandest mosque, and a population exceeding 50,000 people. The city thrived off its remote but convenient location: the pit stop between the great Saharan caravan routes and the Niger River. It was here that men traded salt, painstakingly harvested from the scorching plains of the Sahara, for the gold, ivory, and slaves that came from the south. Slavery would become one of Timbuktu's most lucrative operations, the Arabs giving the Niger the name *Neel el Abeed*, "River of Slaves." However, Africanus would insist that the sale of books from Timbuktu was "more profitable than any other goods." The Saharan city was to Africa what Florence had been to Enlightenment Europe—a place renowned for its scholarly and artistic endeavors, where learning and culture reached a zenith of sophistication during the Songhai Empire's reign from 1463 to 1591.

But unbeknownst to Europeans, this wealth of Timbuktu disappeared after 1591, when an army of Moors and mercenaries crossed the Sahara with the most sophisticated weaponry of the time—cannon and muskets—and sacked the golden city in a single day. It marked the end of Timbuktu's scholarly and entrepreneurial supremacy, beginning a decline from which the city would never recover. Still, ill-informed Europeans embarked, one after the next, for an African El Dorado that didn't exist anymore. There were only two ways to get there, neither very promising: you could risk enslavement or death by trying to cross the great ocean of sand from the north, or brave the malarial jungles of West Africa and then travel up the Niger. Park's journey would usher in the frantic "Timbuctoo Rush" of the early 1800s, and it wasn't long before the "River of Slaves" and its surrounding country came to be known as the "White Man's Grave."

CHAPTER TWO

⤳

IT'S THE MIDDLE OF THE NIGHT AND I WAKE WITH A START: THE BEAR bell on my kayak is ringing—two men have discovered my boat. From inside my tent pitched on shore, I can hear them whispering to each other, the light from their flashlight flickering anxiously about the dark shore. I had hoped that the bell would prove an unnecessary—if not paranoid—precaution on my part, but here we are: the middle of the night, two strange men going through my things, and only a can of mace and some martial arts training between me and potential theft, bodily harm, or both.

I forget about this sort of thing before I go on these trips. Or, more accurately, I ignore the possibility of this sort of thing happening. It's hard when you don't know a place and its people yet. There are no experts to call because no one has done this before, no Lonely Planet guides to consult for precautions when camping alone along the Niger. In this case, I don't even know what tribe I'm dealing with. Fulani or Bambarra? Bozo or Somono? Each has different customs, different points of view. Each wonders why you're here. Usually these issues work themselves out. People tend to be nice and hospitable. Usually. But then my bear bell starts ringing in the middle of the night.

But they don't know that I'm alone. And they don't know that I'm a woman. I could be a big, bad white guy with an attitude. So I get up, arm myself with a section of a kayaking paddle, and burst out of my tent, yelling, "*Hey!*" in a deep, madman's voice.

It works. They flee in their canoe, paddles making a *splunking* sound in the river. I watch in the faint moonlight as they disappear around a bend, sighing in relief, my breath quivering.

But it's not over yet. I hear their voices again. And now I see their flashlight beam coming toward me across the savanna. I run to take down my tent, stuffing things into my kayak wherever they'll fit. In a matter of minutes, I have all my possessions in the boat and shove off. The men reach my camping spot soon after I leave, and they stand on the shore: two dark figures barely distinguishable from the starless night. I paddle hard over the lurid, silver-colored waters, the river nearly a mile wide here and no telling how deep.

I stop after a while, sitting back in my seat, letting the waves pull and tug at my boat. All around me: the lapping quicksilver waters. No sight of land, no suggestion of people. Like experiencing some sort of primordial beginning of the world, the womb of creation. All I have is my little boat, the air within its cavities keeping me afloat in this void. I'm scared to make a sound, as if even a deep breath might somehow disturb the complex machinations of conception. I might be the last person alive in the world, or the first. That's how it feels right now. The thought makes me uneasy, as does the idea of napping on a West African river in the middle of the night. Not surprisingly, sleep won't come, so I just float along to wherever the river wants to take me, wondering what might have happened if I'd stayed on shore. Unpleasant as it is to be floating like this, and tired as I am, I'm convinced I made the right decision by leaving.

When I was young, I wasn't very prudent about anything. I just didn't know any better. I'd take all these outrageous risks. My mother worked as a waitress late into the night, while my father—in his own unfathomable world of depression—sat in his spot on the sofa after work and barely moved or spoke until bedtime. I was left to do whatever I wanted. And I did. Went to places where little girls probably shouldn't have gone. I collected cans at forest preserves for spare change, wandering in the midst of motorcycle gangs having parties, black-leathered folk who shared their beers with me. Budweiser, usually. I raided the dumpsters behind porno shops with my brother, biking off with my booty to sell it to neighborhood boys. Got in fights with those same boys, with lots of boys, gained a reputation for kicking their asses. It was the classic acting-out of childhood, if I look behind all the messiness of past events. Just a desperate need for attention and love that, when unfulfilled, has a way of evolving into fierce independence, tenacity, a drive to take care of oneself at all costs.

Do they stay with us? Those old needs? Are they the mysterious source of wanderlust, the secret ache propelling all journeys? It's tempting to draw too quick a conclusion. Mungo Park was said to be notoriously reserved, a dreamer and lover of romantic poetry. His mind was filled with Scottish ballads, tales of daring, hardship, perseverance. His father wanted him to become a minister, but he chose medicine instead. Those were the days of bleedings with leeches, of using poison to cure. Park adapted himself well to this work but found his interests veered elsewhere, to botany. He obtained a position as surgeon for the East India Company and was soon off to Sumatra, where he busied himself with classifying plants and animals that he found in the jungle. He returned to Scotland after a year, the travel bug having bitten him. He was hopelessly drawn to in the fantastic worlds he had found, regardless of the dangers they might hold.

I get similarly lost in what's out there; every few months I'm hungry for a journey. But I have trouble explaining this to some people. I remember my flight from Paris to Mali. I was sitting next to a Frenchman named Jean who was traveling to Bamako on business. He wore a short-sleeved pastel blue shirt and dress pants, which he was anxiously patting and pulling at as if it were a costume he couldn't wait to take off. He kept smoothing back the graying hair at his temples, gazing through his glasses at the map of the Niger River in my lap. I could see that he'd been wondering about me. And with our flight from Paris nearly over, Mali's capital, Bamako, approaching, he leaned back and turned to me, his voice jarring the silence.

"Are you in the Peace Corps?" he asked. Which is, apparently, the only reason why any Americans go to Mali.

I shook my head. "I'm going to be traveling on the Niger River," I said. "In a kayak."

"A kayak?" he sputtered. "Where will you go?"

"I'm paddling from Ségou to Timbuktu."

"That's very far!"

"Well, it's about 600 miles," I said.

"Will you go alone?"

I nodded.

"Do you know someone who has done this before?" he asked.

"No. As far as I know, I'll be the first."

And Jean felt compelled to lean across the aisle and tell his friend, who looked at me and grinned as he heard the translation in French.

"There are no hotels in the country. When you leave Bamako, there is nothing," his friend said to me. He emphasized the word "nothing" as if we were back in Mungo Park's time, as if he were speaking about great unknown spaces, the Darkest Africa.

"Yeah, I know. I'll be camping," I tell him.

"Camping? But lions!" Jean said.

"I'll also be staying in villages."

"And hippos," his friend added. "There are hippos in the river, and they are very dangerous. Do you know this?"

Hippos I knew about. As a matter of fact, I had a strange, irrational fear of hippos that was so strong it might have come out of a past life. Before my trip, fearing these creatures more than anything else, I called some well-known travel writers, names given to me by the magazine, men in their fifties or sixties who had been everywhere on the globe by now, several times over. What about hippos? I asked them. What does one do about hippos?

They had no suggestions for me. They'd never kayaked through hippo country, and they advised me not to do it either. They advised me about other things, too. *Look,* one person said to me, *you don't want to do this trip without having someone on the ground to tell you what's out there. You need to find out if a village up ahead is going to kill you for your camera.* Which was a very different kind of paternal advice from what my father used to give me when I was growing up—"Lock the door when you leave."

"I'll deal with hippos when they come," I said to the Frenchman.

"Do you think these villages will be safe?" Jean asked.

"I don't know," I said. "Hopefully."

Days before I was supposed to leave, my travel doctor handed me a memo from the U.S. State Department about Mali. Parts of it stood out to me: "female travelers, in particular, have reported being harassed.... Travelers should stay alert, remain in groups, and avoid poorly lit areas after dark.... Corruption is prevalent.... Poorly maintained, overloaded transport and cargo vehicles frequently break down and cause accidents. Undisciplined drivers render traffic movements unpredictable.... Nighttime driving is particularly hazardous as vehicles lack headlights and/or taillights.... Safety of public transportation: poor.... Availability of roadside assistance: poor.... Avoid traveling on Air Mali due to safety concerns.... Visitors should not travel overland to the northern regions.... Banditry is a serious risk.... Travel should be avoided on the left bank of the Niger River and outside major centers."

I anticipated having to break several of those rules, if not all of them. There seemed to be no way of avoiding it. Most obviously, I would definitely need to land on the dreaded left bank of the Niger River, and of course my entire trip was predicated on venturing "outside major centers." Without specific literature, or the skinny from famous travel writers who had been there and done that, what I was about to do was merely a blank screen to put my experiences on. And while I felt fear, I didn't let it become my modus operandi, ruling my life and decisions to the point of immobility. This is the trade-off that I have acknowledged and accepted for my life: I am willing to sacrifice some of my security for the excitement of raw adventure. Which means, of course, that I must be prepared to accept all consequences. And which also means, generally, that my trips have large helpings of the unpleasant side of things.

Fear of danger is a funny thing, too. It tends not to be around when it ought to be; it definitely has an agenda of its own. It's ironic how danger doesn't present itself when we'd expect, but instead creeps and connives to appear when we feel the safest. Before I left on this trip, I was at a Buddhist retreat in rural northwestern Missouri. This was a place of sunny cornfields, of spicy country air smelling of goldenrod and milkweed. I stayed at a Benedictine monastery, brown-robed monks silently wandering the grounds, used to all of us weird Buddhist and tai-chi folk who moved around like zombies outside. You rarely heard the sound of cars there, and the sun set each night in pale red hues over fields that sent armies of fireflies whirling into the dusk. It felt like the safest place I had ever been, which was saying a lot, as I had visited war zones and killing fields and been in the midst of a coup, and I had come to believe that every place is draped in horror, either latent or realized. But here was a place where the front gate hadn't been locked in fifty years, where men prayed over meals and sang hymns of faith and love each night.

Shortly after I left, a lone man, armed with rifles and ammunition, drove through the gate of the monastery. The evening news showed that he parked in the same spot where I had parked, walked casually into the monastery, and fired at everyone he saw. He critically injured two monks and killed another two before walking into the chapel and sitting in the pew where I had sat, no doubt staring at the same painting of Jesus that I had seen, and blowing his brains out.

No place is safe. Safety, itself, is an illusion. And I wonder if it is my deep acceptance of this that makes it easier for me to do these trips. No place is safe. And while I don't advocate tempting fate, I guess I just don't worry much about it, either.

I remember how on that plane with Jean it was dark and raining outside. We descended toward Bamako through thick storm clouds that gave only a shady, fretful view of the landscape below. Jean was holding his head as the plane dipped and rose, letting out soft moans. I didn't see many lights on the ground, nor were there neat displays of houses, or skyscrapers, or highways, or anything familiar. Just a nervous darkness without shape or form. Even the runway appeared like a clumsy trail of lights that strained to be seen through rain and shadow. I felt my heart leap along with the struggling plane, feeling twinges of regret. But it was too late. The journey had caught me, from the minute I got on the plane, and it would take me to whatever end.

I turned to Jean, wanting to keep things lighthearted. "So do you like Mali?" I asked. He was still holding his head in his hands. Our plane carefully visited the runway only to peel into the air at the last minute, to try again.

He sighed and looked at me incredulously. "I prefer France," he said.

⌇

I SIT UP IN MY KAYAK NOW. A LARGE CANOE IS COMING DIRECTLY toward me from the darkness. I take up my paddle and drive myself away, nearly hitting it, and look back to see no one inside. Like a canoe driven by ghosts, the large black vessel disappearing into the moonlight.

I hear the sound of waves now—I seem to be entering some kind of rapid. I secure my things and paddle toward the opposite shore where I see a distant light, not wanting to be on this river anymore when it's dark out. The waves get bigger, barreling at me from the darkness. My kayak hits them head-on, spray showering over me. I know I need to get out of the middle of this immense river, yet I can barely see what I'm facing in front of me. I free my flashlight from my bag and hold it in my teeth as I paddle. *Got to get to the shore, to that light.* The waves keep coming at me, drenching me, the current tugging at my rudder and trying to take control of my boat.

I paddle with all the energy I have left, my injured arm scream-ing in pain. The light on the shore barely seems to get closer. It is the optical illusion of night paddling, the appearance of things as not mov-ing, not getting any closer. I tug even harder at the paddle. And now, at last—it comes closer. And closer still. But what a long night. I'm ready to collapse.

I cut through the fast current and pull toward shore, where I see a dock illuminated by the feeble glow of a kerosene lamp beside a nearby hut. I tie up my kayak, relieved to have arrived safely. A village sleeps nearby; my watch reads 4:12 a.m. I pull myself onto shore, grateful for the solid ground beneath me. Lying down, I wrap my rain poncho around me. I don't care what people are going to think when they wake up and see me like this—I'm too tired to worry about it.

Now is the time when my mind asks what I'm doing here, and why this journey. But such thoughts feel insidious, my injured arm swollen and throbbing, mosquitoes trying to find entry to my skin. I close my eyes to try to sleep.

CHAPTER THREE

~

I STILL FEEL THE NIGHT IN MY MIND, A HEAVINESS THAT FILLS MY WHOLE body and brings a slow labor to my paddle strokes. The Niger is like a sheet of silk around me, the water soft and pliant before even the slightest movement. The shores look verdant and jungle-like, ringing with the sharp, fervent insect calls left over from the night. I watch the sun rising, its clean white light pressing through morning clouds and filling me with peace.

Something is strange and striking about my time on the river now, and it takes me a few moments to figure out what: there are no signs of Western civilization on the shores. No electrical wires, no phone lines, no roads, no cars. No sounds of engines or of planes overhead. The buildings are constructed from earth and thatch, rather than cement, brick, steel. I see only adobe or woven grass mats wherever there are people. And no hotels, restaurants, gas stations, flushing toilets, running water. No electricity whatsoever, or telephones. I couldn't contact anyone even if I wanted to, nor could anyone find me. This must be what is meant by being "on my own." This is what is tantalizing me most about this trip: the necessity of revamping all my requirements and expectations for life, of doing without, of knowing that I need very little to sustain me.

It all amazes me—not a single familiar sight is to be found anywhere along this river. People haul produce as they did thousands of years ago: by donkey cart. They still travel the river in wooden canoes. Motorized boats are entirely absent from the water, with the rare exception of a passing river barge every few days. No one can afford either the outboard or the petrol, let alone the boat, which particularly surprises me—back home, the waterways are filled with people in their own motorboats, who stream by in a display of noise and diesel exhaust. But none of that here, which is why I feel the odd sensation of going back in time.

My experience on the Niger is probably closer to Mungo Park's first journey here than I ever realized. As I float along in my kayak, I pull out his narrative and read some of the passages, having the bizarre feeling of *knowing* exactly what he's talking about, of experiencing exactly the same thing, so that 200 years might have never transpired between our voyages. In one part of his narrative, he wrote about the very country I pass through now:

> "We arrived at Modiboo, a delightful village on the banks of the Niger, commanding a view of the river for many miles, both to the east and west. The small green islands (the peaceful retreat of some industrious Foulahs [Fulani], whose cattle are here secure from the depredations of wild beasts), and the majestic breadth of the river, which is here much larger than at Ségou, render the situation one of the most enchanting in the world. Here are caught a great plenty of fish, by means of long cotton nets, which the natives make themselves."

I have seen those very nets, have seen the catches of fish, the lush islands used as safe grazing grounds. I feel closer to the explorer than I ever thought possible.

Waving at the people I meet becomes a pastime now and has moved from novelty to habit. Back home in Missouri, people don't usually wave at each other. They've forgotten how to do it, or perhaps were never taught. Here, it is perpetual greeting and exchanges of goodwill. And such smiles: the smallest babies transfixed with pleasure to see me in my boat, children whooping and laughing on shore, women grinning. I notice how different we look from each other: I, in my long, patterned skirt, my blond hair and T-shirt, and my Australian bush hat; they in their colorful pagnes, breasts bared, hair in elaborate cornrows woven with rings of pure gold. But as we stare at each other, the differences dissolve. Beyond the confines of sight, there is no division. We share all those things that make us uniquely human—the joys and pains, loss and hope.

The sun rises and clears away the morning mists. I find a wide patch of river with barely a current and sit low in my kayak to try to sleep, feeling no fear—the people here are too gentle to hurt anyone. I wake with a start; I must have been drifting for some time. I forget for a moment where I am and look out at the silver waters, seeing my red kayak beneath me. In my dreaming I'd been elsewhere, in some other unimaginable place. For a moment I have to force the world of Mali into my consciousness. All worlds, it seems, are relative.

I paddle past Somono and Bozo fishing villages. Many of the people in these parts believe in a god of the Niger, and they think it's blasphemous to paddle at night without propitiating him. If so, might that explain my difficulties of last night? Sometimes I like to indulge in these ideas of genies and ghosts, wrathful gods and sorcery. What if? I imagine a world ordered by another intangible realm, with everything

I do aided or thwarted by forces I can't see. I imagine myself as the proverbial pawn in the hand of some greater intelligence, none of the moves my own. The god of the river might toss me in the waves of the Niger, plunge me through storms and rapids, send men after me in the night. I have no say in any of it. This reminds me that far away from Mali's animist roots, in the Far East, many people believe there are no gods. Everything is the result of causes and conditions. Karma. The lives we live and don't live. The things that happen to us in each moment. The kindness and the sufferings we receive. In this sense, there are no accidents or mistakes. Which I find myself rebelling against. I *want* to know that I play some role in outcomes; I *want* to believe that I'm able to dictate where I'm going and what will happen to me. My mind struggles against submitting wholly to the whims of this journey.

As the noonday heat and humidity rise into the mid-90s, according to my thermometer, I keep looking around the next bend for the town of Markala and its incongruous bridge stretching over the Niger—the only such bridge I'll pass all the way to Timbuktu. I feel as if I barely cover any ground, the current so slow and the paddling so long, though I know that impatience is senseless on this trip. I'll get there when I get there. I remind myself that it was this exact stretch of river, during the same season of the year, that had tormented Mungo Park with its heat. "The canoes were not covered with mats," he wrote, "and there being no wind, the sun became insufferably hot. I felt myself affected with a violent headache, which increased to such a degree as to make me almost delirious. I never felt so hot a day; there was sensible heat sufficient to have roasted a sirloin." Through even the highest SPF sunscreen I can see my skin turning red and parched. I've been wearing a skirt over a pair of kayaking shorts, which I pull down whenever canoes approach (women who wear pants in rural Mali—let alone shorts—are viewed as prostitutes), and now I'm glad

I have the skirt to protect my legs as well. Like Park, I can find no escape from this sun.

The bridge appears in the distance, a long steel structure left over from French colonial days; it looks like something aliens might have dropped into the Malian countryside on a whim. Donkey carts loaded with hay travel across its anachronistic metal rungs; women hang up washing on its girders. The current is so slow that the bridge is a very long time coming. When I do finally pass beneath it—my first clear sign of progress achieved—the Niger begins a 180-degree turn west that will circle northeast again. But progress is short-lived out here. For every landmark I get to, there's always the next one, annoyingly distant. And so frustration and impatience set in. I am a student of impatience; I have a hard time waiting for anything. Back home, when working on projects, all I see is the distance I have to go to reach the end; no progress I make ever seems adequate. Here, though, I can only paddle so fast, and river and weather have an agenda of their own. This journey doesn't care what I want to accomplish.

It is a true human curse—that dogged insistence that things go our way. I must stop estimating how far I'll be able to paddle in a single day. My map, when I look at it, must be only for orienting myself. No plans anymore. No objectives other than getting to Timbuktu. I must learn how to stop imposing my demands on the world.

⌒

THE SUN IS STARTING TO SET; I'LL SOON BE ARRIVING AT SANSANDING. My injured right arm is so swollen and painful that paddling has turned into an act of masochism, but doctors and hospitals are two more things that don't exist on this river. I put on a wrist brace I brought from home and try to forget about it.

I can feel my excitement rising at the prospect of seeing Sansanding for the first time. This town is almost as special to me as Timbuktu because Mungo Park was there. He writes about Sansanding in the narratives from both his journeys, and so it feels the closest I'll be able to get to the explorer. In Sansanding, I can actually walk where Park walked, knowing with certainty that our two journeys have finally, undeniably, intersected.

As I pass around the final bend of the Niger, heading due east, I see Sansanding for the first time. The town looks like some vision from a Coleridge poem. It sits far across a sandy floodplain, the white minarets of one of its mosques rising like castle turrets above the heat waves. I feel farther from home than I have ever felt before. I feel like one of the explorers of old, coming upon some secret desert kingdom. As I get closer, I see a collection of brown adobe houses crouching around the great white mosque. Giant, gnarly kapok trees spread branches over the terraced homes. I see a clearing in the middle of the town, filled with empty market stalls. On a high bank sits a graveyard, each plot marked by a tombstone and a flat rock spread on the ground, the graves all facing Mecca. Wooden canoes with pointy ends rest along the shore, where crowds of naked kids play in the water and women do their washing. Everything looks ancient and full of mystery. Here is the epitome of travel to me: being dazed by newness and exoticism, with all previous experience, all former reference points, deserting me utterly.

I paddle round a small bend, approaching Sansanding. The naked children playing in the water spot me and start screaming and jumping around. Women, naked from the waist up and bent over their washing, straighten and gape at me. I wave and say the Bambarra word for hello, *iniché*, and there follows a moment for processing: a lone white woman in a tiny red boat, speaking their language. All at once, they wave enthusiastically to me, and soon well over a hundred people crowd along the shore to await my arrival.

I find it a very unsettling thing to paddle my kayak straight into a crowd so large, so full of excited, yelling, gesticulating people. I have no way of knowing what to expect. Will they greet me warmly? Will they try to pull me from my boat? This town probably never receives tourists. Even the sages at Lonely Planet have failed to give it a sentence or two of mention in their *West Africa* guidebook.

I coast to shore, the rudder scraping on the sandy bottom and lodging me a few feet from dry ground. The crowd surrounds me, with kids squeezing forward to touch my kayak. They reach out their hands tentatively, as if the boat might blow up in their faces. I have never been in the midst of such a big, tight mass of people. I look at them and see fear, shyness, excitement in their faces. I greet them in French and then in Bambarra, and they smile to hear their own language spoken.

"Where are you going, miss?" one man asks me in French.

"To Timbuktu."

"In this boat?" He steps forward to survey it, squeezing the hull with his hand and holding my paddle. "That's not possible," he concludes.

He translates to everyone what I told him, that I intend to paddle all the way to Timbuktu in what he considers a pathetic sham of a boat, and the women touch fingertips to foreheads, muttering, "*Eh, Allah.*"

I try to get out of the boat, but the kids are too thick around me. They press against the kayak, fighting with each other to have the privilege of touching the shiny red skin of the hull. Finally, fortunately, a man with a wooden switch comes forward and drives them away, and I'm able to get out of my kayak.

My experience here is nearly identical to Mungo Park's. "We

reached Sansanding at ten o'clock," he wrote. "Such crowds of people came to shore to see us, that we could not land our baggage till the people were beaten away with sticks." Ironically, Park chose Sansanding for the official start of his second trip because he believed it would offer him a respite from the gaping crowds at Old Ségou. But Sansanding would prove just as troublesome.

Park described his first trip here in his narrative *Travels in the Interior Districts of Africa*, and the experience had been anything but pleasant. Sansanding in 1797 was one of the Niger River's premier slave-trading destinations, inhabited by Moors and black African traders. Even back then, Sansanding was a large place, with roughly 9,000 inhabitants. Park had been the first European to ever set foot there and had subsequently been the source of much curiosity and alarm. At that time, too, Park was nearly destitute and had only the 5,000 cowries (used as money in these parts) that Mansong, king of Bambarra, had given him in an attempt to get the cumbersome white man to leave Ségou. Consequently, Park found himself entirely dependent on native hospitality.

For me, it is much the same scenario, except that I'm not destitute as I have National Geographic Society expense money. I must still find someone willing to put me up for the night. I decide to do what Park did. He had learned to follow the local custom of finding the chief of the town, giving him a large gift, and asking him for permission to lodge in town. I'm a bit wary of trying this myself, though, because Park's first experience here had been anything but agreeable:

> I was surrounded with hundreds of people, speaking
> a variety of different dialects, all equally unintelligi-
> ble to me.... The Moors now assembled in great
> number; with their usual arrogance, compelling the

Negroes to stand at a distance. They immediately began to question me concerning my religion [insisting that] I must conform so far as to repeat the Mahomedan prayers; and when I attempted to waive the subject, by telling them that I could not speak Arabic, one of them ... started up and swore by the Prophet, that if I refused to go to the mosque, he would be the one that would assist in carrying me thither.... They compelled me to ascend a high seat, by the door of the mosque, in order that every body might see me; for the people had assembled in such numbers as to be quite ungovernable; climbing upon the houses, and squeezing each other, like the spectators at an execution. Upon this seat I remained until sunset.

Poor Mungo, I thought when I read that passage, and I think it now as I try to maneuver through the pressing, jostling crowd in search of the *doogootigi*, or chief.

Park's second visit to Sansanding saw him less destitute, but surely more despondent. This was where he spent weeks with the last of his original 44 soldiers, trying to get some canoes from Mansong so that he could fashion himself a boat for travel down the Niger. With his carpenters all dead, it took him a while to construct his H.M.S. *Joliba*. I can already imagine what it was like for him: the weeks of wiping sweat from his face and pounding and sanding away, while crowds of naked children stood at arm's length, watching, having no place to go and nothing better to do. Park would have provided unrelenting entertainment for the town's citizens; I wonder if villages had even identified a particular year in their history: the Coming of the

Crazy White Man. In fact, European travelers coming after him discovered that Park's name had made it into the songs and oral history of these parts. The words to one such song, sung by a group of women with whom Park had stayed in Old Ségou, went as follows:

"The winds roared, and the rains fell. The poor white man, faint and weary, came and sat under our tree. He has no mother to bring him milk; no wife to grind his corn. Let us pity the white man; no mother has he."

On his second journey, Park actually intended to reach the termination of the Niger itself (a thousand miles from Sansanding), so he needed to make sure his boat was strong, functional, and fully equipped with supplies. This careful attention to construction and outfitting took so much time that his few remaining soldiers started to die off from illness, and, though he was personally opposed to slavery, Park saw no choice but to buy a few slaves to help man his boat.

Slavery is a touchy subject in Park's narrative. At the time he left on his trips, England had not yet abolished slavery (which wouldn't happen until 1807) and was still a major participant in the transatlantic trade in human lives, which was one of the most profitable activities a person could be engaged in. A single British ship could expect to earn upwards of a hundred thousand in pounds sterling per shipment of slaves—an unimaginably enormous sum at that time. Still, British abolitionists made headway in the political debate much sooner than their American counterparts, and the trade was becoming less and less acceptable in England. Park found himself writing his narrative at a time when tempers were high on both sides of the debate, and perhaps for this reason he never openly denounced the slave trade in his writing, a fact that has angered some modern critics of his work. But biographers have suggested that Park probably wrote antislavery comments in his narrative's original draft, only to have the parts cut out or changed by editors more concerned about profits than principle: criticizing the slave trade would have hurt book sales. It is entirely possible, too, that Park, badly wanting a commission from the British government for a new expedition, decided it wasn't in his best interests to make political enemies.

As Park would point out, West Africa had enjoyed a long tradition of slavery, the institution firmly established in all the regions he traveled through. Park estimated that "persons of free condition ... constitute, I suppose, not more than one-fourth part of the inhabitants at large; the other three-fourths are in a state of hopeless and hereditary slavery; and are employed in cultivating the land, in the care of cattle, and in servile offices of all kinds, much in the same manner as the slaves of the West Indies." The Arab and European slave trades greatly exacerbated the problem by providing local slave traders with the most lucrative and unquenchable market for slaves yet, with millions of black Africans being shipped to North African and Middle Eastern harems, as well as to the Americas along the infamous Middle Passage. The European hunger for slaves was so great that West Africans widely believed that the white men considered African people a delicacy and were shipping them away in order to eat them. Park wrote, "[The slaves] repeatedly asked if my countrymen were cannibals. They were very desirous to know what became of the slaves after they had crossed the salt water.... [It] is a deeply rooted idea that the whites purchase Negroes for the purpose of devouring them."

To this day, de facto slavery still exists in Mali, up in the north around Timbuktu. Malian officials and anthropologists often deny this, though, saying that slavery was officially abolished. Still, thousands of people—black-African Bella people—work for Arab masters as unpaid laborers, unable to end their servitude for myriad economic, social, and psychological reasons. If and when I get to Timbuktu, I will find out the truth for myself. I carry two gold coins from home, thinking I might try to free someone with them.

It's impossible for me to view these ancient streets of Sansanding without imagining the thousands of slaves who passed through on their way to the West African coast and European ships. When Park was here, slavery seemed to have reached its height, a fact that thoroughly disgusted him. Though his narrative tries to be politically inoffensive, Park still goes out of his way to describe the brutality of the trade, openly sympathizing with the plight of the enslaved people he encounters on his journeys. Penniless and trying to return to the coast at the end of his first journey, Park accepted the invitation to travel with a slave caravan, or "coffle" as they were called, for the security it would provide him from bandits. In one chapter, he described at length the fate of a woman slave with whom he had journeyed:

> The woman slave ... whose name was Nealee, was not come up [and] they found [her] lying by the rivulet. She was very much exhausted, [refusing] to proceed any farther; declaring that she would rather die than walk another step. As entreaties and threats were used in vain, the whip was at length applied.... Though she was unable to rise, the whip was a second time applied, but without effect; upon which Karfa [the leader of the coffle] desired two of the slatees [slavers] to place her upon the ass which carried our dry provisions [and] the woman was carried forward until dark.... At daybreak poor Nealee was

awakened; but her limbs were now become so stiff and painful, that she could neither walk nor stand; she was therefore lifted, like a corpse, upon the back of the ass.... [S]he was quickly thrown off, and had one of her legs much bruised. Every attempt to carry her forward being thus found ineffectual, the general cry of the coffle was, *kang-teri, kang-teri,* "cut her throat, cut her throat"; an operation I did not wish to see performed, and therefore marched onwards with the foremost of the coffle. The sad fate of this wretched woman made a strong impression.

Park reached the West African coast with this slave coffle, concerned about the fate of the slaves with whom he had traveled so far and so long. He wrote:

Although I was now approaching the end of my tedious and toilsome journey, and expected, in another day, to meet with countrymen and friends, I could not part, for the last time, with my unfortunate fellow-travellers, doomed, as I knew most of them to be, to a life of captivity and slavery in a foreign land, without great emotion.... [T]hese poor slaves, amidst their own infinitely greater sufferings, would commiserate mine; and frequently, of their own accord, bring water to quench my thirst, and at night collect branches and leaves to prepare me a bed in the Wilderness. We parted with reciprocal expressions of regret and benediction. My good wishes and prayers were all I could bestow upon them; and it afforded me some consolation to be told, that they were sensible I had no more to give.

This is the Mungo Park I'm searching for on this journey, the man I so often admire. And pity.

I ask the crowd in clunky Bambarra where I might find the chief. A man leads me up some clay steps toward a terraced courtyard. The town is built on a high bank, with winding layers of adobe homes creating narrow, rising passageways. It occurs to me that I've arrived in a less than presentable state: muddy clothes, red and perspiring face, filthy sandals held together with plastic ties, my Australian bush hat collapsed at a strange angle upon my head. I take off my hat and smooth down my hair, wiping mud from my T-shirt. I haven't been traveling by myself long enough to shed the burden of worrying about another's gaze.

I'm led in front of an older man wearing a long, pink robe that reaches his knees, called a *grand bubu* in Mali, with baggy pants and matching pink fez. He lounges on a mat in the shade of a large tree, watching me with displeasure. I straighten my skirt, which sits lopsided over my kayaking shorts, and greet him.

"This is the chief," a young man who speaks French tells me. "His name is Badulai."

The chief frowns at me, swatting flies from his face and fondling a string of prayer beads. Suddenly, he speaks imperiously to me in Bambarra. The entourage around him studies me closely, and the man with the French steps forward.

"The chief wants a gift from you," he tells me.

"Right." I had known this request would come, though I wasn't sure at what point during the interview. *Give out the bucks as soon as possible,* I note to myself, as I stick a hand down my skirt into a pocket of my shorts. The chief is frowning and turning his head away, as if I were doing something dirty. I pull out a bill and give it to him. It is a large bill, a generous sum by Malian standards, and the chief seems pleased, his frown receding into a light scowl. Being a chief in these villages is a hereditary honor; I don't see anything further qualifying them. I ask him if I can spend the night in Sansanding, and he nods, telling a man to guide me to the place where I can stay.

They put me up with the town English teacher, Yaya Fomba, a man whose English is so poor that I can barely understand him. I frequently look to his young wife, Yakiri, for French translations. Yakiri is about half Yaya's age and was a former pupil of his. I can see why Yaya was attracted to her—she is robust, attractive, has the kind of wide, benevolent smile that makes you feel immediately at ease. She wears a colorful red-patterned pagne, her hair wrapped up in cloth of the same color. Even the casual dress of women in Mali shows great attention to fashion and elegance, and I feel self-consciously grubby in my sweat-stained T-shirt and wet skirt.

When Yaya hears I'm paddling to Timbuktu, he loses his English for a moment. "*Incroyable*," he says. "Unbelievable."

Yakiri shakes her head and sighs. "*Eh, Allah*," she says. "You are crazy! Take the bus."

We laugh. I rub my injured arm, unable to lift anything with it. Crazy indeed, to be at the beginning of such a long trip with a problematic injury. But I'm as averse to quitting as Park was. I'm determined to get to Timbuktu.

I leave Yaya's house to take a look around Sansanding, trying to find the mosque where Park was on display for the crowds. The dirt streets send up mini-tornadoes of dust and garbage every time the wind blows through town. There is the robust smell of wood ash, the acrid sweetness of decaying fruit and garbage. White doves alight on the mud-brick houses, sidestepping past lizards and bobbing on the edges of the roofs, watching me. I pass the town garbage dump, a deep crater where skeletal donkeys and goats scavenge for scraps. Hens walk in stilted deliberation through the refuse, heads nodding, packs of frantic chicks stumbling in their wake. Adobe homes have grown up around the dump, circling to its very edges, little naked kids playing on the fringe. Sansanding, I've been told by Yaya, is a prosperous town. I'm wondering what a not-so-prosperous town would look like.

I pass some sheep tied to a tree and stop to touch their noses. The children nearby stare at me and giggle: sheep aren't for petting; they're for eating. I head toward the market, where Mungo traded away the last of his European goods for provisions for his final journey on the Niger. The wooden stalls lie empty, overrun with the omnipresent donkeys and goats, but from the area's sheer size, I can tell it's a hectic place on market day—and has been, ever since Park's time. "The market is crowded with people from morning to night," Park wrote. "Some of the stalls contain nothing but beads; others indigo in balls; others woodashes.... In houses fronting the square is sold scarlet, amber, silks from Morocco, and tobacco, which comes by way of Timbuctoo. Adjoining this is the salt market, part of which occupies one corner of the square. A slab of salt is sold commonly for eight thousand cowries." Salt is still valuable, is sold in Malian markets in the shape of large gray slabs that resemble tombstones. It all reminds me that what I find most interesting about a place and its history are not the things that have changed, but what's remained the same.

During one of his lonely, crowd-infested days in the market of Sansanding, Park experienced the greatest blow to his spirits: the death of Alexander Anderson, his brother-in-law and good friend who had accompanied him all the way from Scotland. Park noted the death in his journal:

"My dear friend Mr. Alexander Anderson died after a sickness of four months. I feel much inclined to speak of his merits; but as his worth was known only to a few friends, I will rather cherish his memory in silence, and imitate his cool and steady conduct, than weary my friends with a panegyric in which they cannot be supposed to join. I shall only observe that no event which took place during the journey ever threw the smallest gloom over my mind, till I laid Mr. Anderson in the grave. I then felt myself as if left a second time lonely and friendless amidst the wilds of Africa."

I look up and down the shore, wondering if Anderson had been buried beneath these sandy banks, or up in the cemetery beneath the ancient trees. Park must have chosen a good spot for him, out of the sun.

I catch sight of a small mosque nearby, and I go to see how old it is, to see if it could be the one where Mungo Park was surrounded by the crowds. I see a young man by the gate, wearing a long white shirt and embroidered fez. I ask him if I can come inside the gate to look at the mosque.

"No, no," he says. "You are a *tubab*—a white person." He shakes his head and laughs with such amusement that I feel as if I've missed the punch line of some joke. "It's forbidden for you."

He tells his friends about my request, as if it were the most outrageous thing he'd ever heard. They all laugh uproariously.

"*C'est interdit,*" one of his friends chimes in. "Not allowed. You are white."

Like being excluded from some little boys' playhouse.

I go to visit the other mosque, the largest one with the high white minarets that seems to be the oldest in Sansanding. It's right on the edge of town, facing the river. The caretaker tells me that this mosque was built in 1766, and I get a feeling that it's the right one—Mungo's mosque. I imagine him sitting in its shade with the crowds all around him, gaping at him with his red hair and European dress. For me, fortunately, only small crowds gather. Women with babies wrapped in cotton cloth, slung on their backs. Little boys sporting mohawks: the haircuts mean they've been named after a particular Muslim saint.

"Hey, Mungo," I say to the mosque. The doves on its roof bob fitfully. "Mun-go."

I don't ask if I can go inside the gate.

CHAPTER FOUR

⤳

MY DAYS ARE FILLED NOW WITH THE SLOW PROGRESSION OF ONE passed village after the next, one outcropping of palm trees after another to break up the monotony of sand and shore. At each village the people greet me with waves and exclamations, and I've never met friendlier folk in my life. The women, in particular, cheer me on, yelling out accolades for *"les femmes fortes,"* strong women, which surprises and delights me. Malian women are themselves an underclass, relegated to purely domestic pursuits, 70 percent of them illiterate. According to various health organizations, at least 90 percent of them have their clitorises and external genitalia completely removed by the time they're teenagers—one of the highest rates in the world.

It is a cottage industry here, clitoridectomies, as well as excision (removal of the labia), and infibulation (complete removal of all external genitalia and the sewing up of the vaginal opening except for a tiny hole the size of a match head through which she must urinate and menstruate). The procedure is generally done by a specially appointed person in the village, who, under typically unsanitary conditions, uses a razor blade or other sharp object to slice off and completely scrape away all of the girl's external genitalia, labia, and clitoris. There is no anesthesia, so the writhing girl must be held down by several adults. When the procedure is finished, the girl's vagina is sewn shut, her legs are tightly tied together, and she is forced to lie on her side for several weeks until the two sides of her vagina heal together. And this is only the physical trial. While some people maintain that these women willingly and gratefully accept their fate, firsthand accounts collected from them largely debunk this notion. Published testimonies from Malian women speak of both physical and psychological trauma. Many grappled with the question of why their parents—those who were supposed to care for them and keep them safe—allowed them to be put through such a tortuously painful procedure. In other cases, the women were subjected to it against the will of their female relatives, with the father or brother forcing them to get the procedure done. What sort of imprint this must leave on their minds and hearts—and on the communal soul of all women—is beyond measure.

There's a law against female genital mutilation in Mali, but no one pays much attention. Through these procedures, men are ensured a virgin at the time of marriage, when the woman's sealed vagina must be cut open for him. And if a jealous husband should happen to be going away for a period of time, he might insist that his wife be sewn back up again until he gets back. The resulting scar tissue and reduction of the vaginal opening means that both sexual intercourse and childbirth are exceedingly painful and difficult for her, yet this is the part no one talks about. Instead, women are taught that their very femininity and fertility are at stake, and so that undesirable, unnecessary little appendage and its surrounding tissue must be removed at all costs.

The practice occurs among Malians of all religions. Among the more animist tribes like the Dogon, women are led to believe that they will remain in a sort of purgatory between man and woman until the "little penis" is cut off. To them, having a clitoris is the antithesis of being a woman; the woman who still has hers remains hopelessly androgynous. Though the removal of the clitoris or external genitalia predates the introduction of Islam in West Africa, it has nonetheless been adopted most widely by Muslims as a way to keep women chaste. Mali enjoys the classic double standard typical of misogynistic cultures—that a man may enjoy his sexual freedom, enjoy the sexual act itself, but a woman cannot. Malian men have told me that they consider the removal of a girl's clitoris a *favor*, a way to protect her from her own dangerous sexual urges. Better to obviate her sexual drives altogether, for her own good. After all, a woman's role is one of childbearing and motherhood, nothing more.

It's been hard for me to go to these villages when I know that most of the women I see have had their clitorises and labia sliced off, their vaginas sewn shut with cat gut. I have trouble holding back my anger. Back in Old Ségou, the Bambarra village where I first began my river trip, the girls have the procedure done at the ripe age of sixteen. *Sixteen.* By that time, presumably, the psychological trauma and physical pain is enormous. And it's not just the ordeal of the practice that I mourn; it's the ensuing medical complications that follow women for the rest of their lives. Chronic bladder infections, difficult and painful urination and menstruation, fibroids, sterility— even death.

Some Western apologists and postcolonial theorists still euphemistically call this procedure "female circumcision" (as if it were a quaint initiation into womanhood and nothing more, equivalent to the removal of a male's foreskin). Furthermore, I have heard such individuals lambasting Western concern or involvement, claiming that any Westerner who cares about the welfare of women in Africa can only be operating from a manipulative or patronizing colonialist stance. This is patently absurd. Basic humanistic interests and concern for women's health seem reason enough for Westerners *and* non-Westerners—men and women alike—to care and become involved in defeating this practice. Assitan Diallo, one of Mali's foremost advocates for the banning of female genital mutilation, explains what role she believes Westerners should have in this issue: "We should keep in mind that many Westerners have more experience in dealing with the subject than we do, because they were the first to talk about it. And now we are also talking about it…. But I don't think I can be in the same group with them to fight something in my own country, because I will feel, 'Here they go again, colonization.' … So in my view, they can be like advisers."

I paddle past the occasional village, waving back at the women doing their washing in the river, comforted by their cheers for me, their interest in my journey as a lone woman. I answer the men's questions, tell them where I'm going and enjoy the stunned looks on their faces when they hear, "Timbuktu." In virtually all ways, I'm completely defying the traditional paradigm of a Malian woman: I don't have a man accompanying me; I do the paddling myself; I am self-sufficient and answer to no one.

⌣

I DECIDE TO SPEND THE NIGHT IN A VILLAGE, AND I PADDLE TO THE only one I can see on a barren stretch of river. It's a collection of a few round adobe huts, topped with thatch. Some women, large washtubs balanced on their heads, see me as I paddle over, and they run off to alert the village. Pretty soon, everyone who can walk, run, or crawl is awaiting me on shore.

I learn that this village is called Seerangoro. The women all wear large gold discs in their earlobes, the older women having several piercings up and down each ear. They style their hair in beautiful, elaborate cornrows with tufts of hair sticking up on top. Their skin is lighter-colored, a dark blue tattoo accentuating the area around the mouth. They bare their breasts with wonderful nonchalance, brightly patterned pagnes covering the areas that Malians consider sexual: the legs and buttocks. They tell me they're Fulani—herders—and I can see their cows grazing nearby, baying for the coming dusk.

Some African scholars believe that the Fulani migrated here many hundreds of years ago from the area near the Red Sea, bringing their herding ways to the Niger and other parts of West Africa. Their lives are inseparable from their cattle, which provide, in addition to milk and meat, a pastoral livelihood that enables them to survive without having to depend on fishing—unlike the Bozo or Somono. It is an independence that makes them wealthy, compared to many rural Malians. A single one of their cows, worth anywhere from $320 to $400, can sustain an entire family for more than a year.

The Fulani are also separated from their Malian compatriots by their appearance. Their light skin suggests Arab origins, and thus they associate themselves with the North Africans who brought writing and scholarship to West Africa, as well as organized religion. The Fulani are considered Mali's most pious tribal group, Islam playing a large role in their lives. It is a distinction in which they take pride, but is often a source of contempt from other indigenous peoples.

The Fulani children stroke my kayak and stare at me. No one speaks a word of French, so I use some of the Bambarra I've learned. I ask them if they can bring me to the *doogootigi*, or chief, knowing from my experience in Sansanding that village etiquette along the Niger hasn't changed much over the centuries: you must always find the doogootigi, give him a gift for visiting his village, and ask him if he'll let you spend the night. Following this procedure is crucial, as it secures his hospitality and patronage, and thus ensures your safety.

I'm led to the chief. He's an old, hunched man who wears a grand smile. We shake hands. I pay him generously, and through a smattering of Bambarra and signs, ask if I can spend the night. He quickly says yes, and instructs the kids to help bring my bags up to the village. They fight with each other to have the privilege of carrying up the kayak itself, the red boat held aloft by scores of little hands. As it only weighs twenty-three pounds, they easily hold it above their heads, cheering as if in a victory celebration, and place it beside the chief's hut. The same thing had happened at Sansanding—I returned from my walk around town to find my kayak safely deposited in Yaya's living room. I find it strange that none of the village people are comfortable leaving my kayak tied in the Niger beside their canoes, but must carry it to the village for safekeeping. Not that anyone would steal or damage it; rather, I think they consider it such a strange and valuable object that it must be kept close at hand.

The women crowd around me, holding up a single finger and speaking in fervent Bambarra. I'm unsure what the finger means, until one woman says two words in their language that I recognize: "husband" and "where?" I gesture to them that I'm alone. This they cannot believe. They point to the river, then to me, holding up a finger again and pretending to paddle.

I nod. Yes. Alone.

One woman named Ba claps her hands and grins. "Alone," she says, like a sigh. She turns to her friends and repeats the word.

The chief's wife comes over with an enormous gourd bowl, full of foaming cow's milk, straight from the udder. Growing up in a Chicago suburb, this is the closest I've ever come to country living. I tentatively sniff the milk. It even *smells* like a cow, which for some reason surprises me, but I lift the bowl and start to drink, and discover it to be delicious.

I take out of the kayak some uncooked rice I bought in Ségou and some fresh fish I bought from a Bozo fisherman, showing them to the women, telling them I'd like to offer them to the village for dinner. They assume I know how to prepare and cook these things because I'm a woman, so they bring out a cooking pot and various implements. I amuse them with my ineptitude. I stare at the rice, the women waiting for me to do something with it. When I put some in the cooking pot, they look at each other, suppressing laughs: I must *clean* the rice first—don't I know this? One woman takes over, showing me how to inspect the rice for impurities before washing it several times in a bowl. Finished, she hands it back to me. Now I put the rice in the cooking pot, but the women are laughing again: I must get water to a *boil* first. They're patient with me, fascinated by my inability to accomplish even the most basic of domestic tasks. And how to explain that I don't know how to cook very well, that I've spent my life in the States, living on ramen noodles and macaroni and cheese? I'd make a lousy wife out here.

I look with apprehension at the fish. I know I must somehow gut them and remove the scales, but, admittedly, I've never done this before. My family never took me fishing; having never fished themselves. I buy my fish precut in little Styrofoam containers in the Wal-Mart meat department. I take out my Swiss Army knife and start puncturing one of the fish bellies. The women are laughing uproariously now: I must take the scales off first. So I try to do so with the knife, but make such a mess of it that again one of the women takes over. She uses a blunt stick to remove them quickly and gently, then guts each fish, throwing the innards to nearby dogs.

We stuff ourselves on rice, listening to West African music on a transistor radio. Little kids dance to the beat, shuffling their bodies and sidestepping. They love music and dance here, each person trying to better the other's moves. In the midst of it, the grandparents spread out on mats with blankets over their heads, snoring loudly. One woman brings out a treasured page she's kept from a French magazine, which shows an advertisement of a white woman reclining on a luxurious bed with pink satin sheets. They point to the photo and then to me, as if that woman and I were somehow related.

Do they think I recline on pink satin sheets back home, in a flowing gown of silk, living a life of such luxury and ease? Do they see all white women in such a way: the Peace Corps person who comes by once a year, the anthropologist, the aid worker? I have no language in common with them, no means of explaining otherwise. I am trapped in the image they have of me, in that room with the satin sheets.

The women want to know many things from me. First of all, where is my husband, and why did he let me paddle on the Niger all by myself? They also want to know how many babies I have back home in America. I try my best to explain through signs and broken Bambarra why none of these things apply, but it takes some time, so that we're still discussing it long after dinner. I'm afraid we might be discussing it all night, but the women at last grow satisfied and declare it's bedtime.

We all lie down side-by-side on foam mattresses spread outside the huts. Mosquito nets stretch overhead, blurring the stars. Fleas hop on my skin; chickens jump on us. I fall asleep to the sound of the old folks' snoring, goats nibbling at our feet.

ALWAYS, IN THE MIDST OF THESE KINDS OF TRIPS, I REACH A POINT
when I suddenly wake up to the reality of what I'm doing. I discover,
quite unexpectedly, that I am alone in a little red boat, paddling a river
in the South Sahara en route to Timbuktu. This becomes news to me,
as if it had all been unreal until now, and I'm forced to pull over to ponder the implications for the first time. Inevitably, I pull out my map.
It tells me that I'm now past the town of Massina, and that my goal
of Timbuktu rests so far to the northeast that it actually hides on
another section of the map.

My God, I think, but always when it's too late. Always when, as is
the case now, a crowd of at least 50 children are running over a nearby
hill and descending upon my boat.

"*Tubabu! Donnez-moi cadeau!*" they scream. "Hey, Whitey! Give me
a gift!"

Their excitement turns chaotic. Hands are everywhere, pulling
and grabbing at the things in my kayak. I take out a bag of dried pineap-
ple slices and throw them in the air, and the mass of bodies shoots
toward the treats, kids fighting and tearing at each other. I have never
seen anything like it, though I tend to think I've seen it all, and I paddle away as if for my life.

I wonder when Mungo Park's moment of realization struck. When he
was captured by the Moors and a woman threw urine in his face? When
he was so destitute that he was forced to sell locks of his hair for good luck
charms? Or perhaps it hadn't come until the second and last journey, when
he left on his river trip in a rotting boat, in the company of his four remaining soldiers, one of whom had gone insane. "Though all the Europeans
who are with me should die, and though I were myself half-dead," Park
wrote in his final letter, "I would still persevere; and if I could not succeed
in the object of my journey, I would at least die on the Niger." *Why did-
n't he turn back?* the reader must wonder. *What was wrong with the man?*

But I am starting to learn more about Park than ever before. I'm starting to understand. Once the journey starts, there's no turning back. That's just the way it is. The journey binds you; it kidnaps and drugs you. It deceives you with images of the end, reached at long last. You picture yourself arriving on that fabled shore. You see everything you promised for yourself. For Park, it might have been streets of gold, cool oasis pools, maidens cooing in his ear. For me, it is much simpler: french fries and air-conditioning.

I paddle around a bend and see a village up ahead that's crowded with people. It's market day there, and large canoes line up along the shore, one after the next, so that there's barely a free space. Market day is a weekly occurrence in nearly every Malian village of any size, and it falls on a different day of the week depending on where you are. This is the first market I've actually witnessed, and so I decide to paddle over to it to see it for myself.

This decision is not without a heady dose of fear. This part of Mali never sees white people, and certainly not a white woman in a kayak. I'm already anticipating the great commotion my arrival will cause. And it's strange, too, to be paddling across the river as if from nowhere, no tour guide accompanying me to explain my appearance, no one to translate. Just me. Going peacefully to the market to try to buy some mangoes, as if there were nothing out of the ordinary about it.

The people don't notice me until I'm nearly to the shore, their attention fixed on the market proceedings. One young boy spots me now and lets out a wail so loud that it could startle a deaf person.

"*Tubab! Tubaaaab!*" he screams. "White person! White person!"

And the cry becomes part of a universal exclamation. *White person!* The reception I'm receiving is not to be believed. Hundreds of people rush to the shore, to the very edge of the ten-foot-high clay embankment that borders the river. They all stare directly at me—

this crowd easily dwarfs the huge reception I had at Sansanding. Children are so keen on having a look at me that they scramble down the clay bank, clinging to tree roots to get a good view. Women smile at me in sheer amazement. The volume of the crowd nearly knocks me from my boat.

"*Tu-baaab! Tu-baaab! Tu-baaaaab!*"

I sense no hostility here whatsoever, just unabashed curiosity. I smile at everyone, greet them in Bambarra with an excited "*Iniche!*"

The minute I speak, the crowd falls silent. Everyone looks at each other, stares back at me, and suddenly they laugh uproariously. It's too much: A lone white woman appearing out of nowhere, speaking their language. They can't seem to fathom it. No one, I notice, speaks a shred of French. But for the smattering of Bambarra words I've learned, I would be unable to communicate with them at all.

I ask what village this is, and either my Bambarra is faulty or their amazement prevents them from understanding, but they look at me in rapt incomprehension and say nothing. I try again. And again, until at last a young boy makes sense of my gestures and announces that I've reached the village of Tuara.

I ask what people live here and get a mixed reply: "Malaka," "Fulani," "Bozo," "Bambarra"—even "Tuareg." I try to be matter-of-fact about my visit, nonchalantly stepping out of my kayak and tying it between some canoes. I hoist my little daypack to my back and stare up at the assemblage of people. The women are dazzling in their colorful sarongs and head-wrappings, the more wealthy among them sporting earrings and head decorations made of pure gold. Some wear their hair in a single braid down either side of their heads, gold rings woven into the locks. Some of them have their mouth areas tattooed dark blue and wear thick gold bands through the septa of their noses. They are a stunning, vibrant people.

Usually when I arrive in the midst of such crowds there will be someone who is especially calm and eager to come to my assistance. In this case, it is a woman with a radiant smile and a scarf of blue silk wrapped about her head. She smiles benevolently at me and encourages me to come up the embankment. I look back at my kayak with all my things inside, worried that something might be taken during my absence, but she merely smiles at me as if she knows what my concerns are. She shakes her head as if to say, "Don't worry," and trusting her implicitly, I start to climb the mud bank. When I slip, the entire crowd acknowledges it in a single loud grunt of concern. Hands reach out to help me up, and soon everyone presses close to me to touch my skin and hair, to stare at my face, my blue eyes. I stare back at the faces, just as amazed to be so close to them. I stare at the dark blue tattoos of the Malaka people, the bright gold nose bands, the smooth brown skin and welcoming eyes.

I can barely move without stepping on someone's foot, so my benefactor with the blue headscarf says a few magic words to the crowd that cause them to move back from me. I head toward the market to see what there is to be seen. Some Tuareg men—a North African Berber people, far from their traditional lands farther north in Mali—leave their stalls to get a better look at me. They're the first Tuareg I've seen in person, are completely cloaked in dark purple indigo wrappings save for hazel eyes that peer out at me. They carry swords strapped to their waists, and stand proudly with their arms crossed, inspecting me.

The market is full of various services and wares: shoe repair, kola nuts, dates, seed pods of various sorts, cooking pots, silverware. I see mangoes for sale and head over to the woman, a large group of people following in my wake. The mangoes cost a trifle—seven cents apiece. I can tell from the price that the stallholders here never see white people, let alone tourists; the going tourist price for a mango in Ségou was sixty cents. I buy several of the fruit, telling the woman to keep the change, and as I deposit them inside my backpack, children take turns petting my arms and stroking my hair. Other children, though, are scared to approach, and I think of something Park wrote: "A few women and children expressed great uneasiness at being so near a man of such an uncommon appearance." Indeed, I must look like some apparition to the youngest kids, many of whom may have never seen a white person before.

I pass through the market for a while, admiring the clay pots that the local women make, enjoying such unusual company all around me. I never know what perception a particular village will have about me, but when they accept me, as this one had (and as the Fulani did the previous night), the experience is pure delight. I forget my usual fears of paddling through an unfamiliar country, alone. All I can think about is how extraordinary this world and its people are.

I return to my kayak. It's where I left it, its contents unmolested, though it has been retied closer to shore for better protection between two large canoes. Children, half-submerged in the river, finger the kayak's rubber skin. They look up at me, grinning nervously as I approach as if I've caught them being naughty. I just smile at them. My benefactor with the silken scarf shakes my hand as I bid her goodbye.

"Where are you going?" she asks in Bambarra.

"To Timbuktu," I say.

"To Timbuktu?! Eh!" She turns to the crowd and announces this information in a shout, and the whole crowd cheers. Just one big blast of voices.

Everyone lines up along the bank to watch me leave—such colorful, gracious people. I untie my kayak and get in, yelling thank you and goodbye in Bambarra. The crowd responds with arms held aloft, hands waving. Just hundreds of people, waving and cheering me on. I paddle off, and it's a while before the last boy stops running after me along the bank, bidding me a fervent farewell.

⟳

I'VE BEEN PADDLING FOR DAYS NOW, STAYING AT VILLAGES, AND AT last some familiarity greets me: Rémi, the magazine photographer covering my trip. He waits in a large *pinasse*, or river barge, that's docked by the town of Diafarabé. He waves and calls me over, aiming at my face an enormous telephoto lens that looks like a bazooka. I feel the old self-consciousness emerging. I've gotten used to being alone. Just me and the world, meeting anew at every turn. And now it's as if the glorious reunion has ended. I'm being pulled back to some reality I thought I'd left behind in a previous life—a reality of magazine issues and photography concerns. To me, it's like a sudden invasion of privacy. Still, I know I'll barely see him on this trip. He has orders to follow me downstream, take some pictures, and then promptly disappear again for days. It's the best compromise I could hope for.

I straighten my hat and smooth back my hair. I think of all the sunscreen smeared on my face, and of the sun-scorched redness of my cheeks. Self-consciousness is a strange, insidious disease. I would have thought I'd have abandoned it by now, makeup free as I am, mud-smeared, greasy-haired, flea-bitten. But here it comes, with a power of its own, telling me that I'm not prepared for having the image of my face transferred onto countless rolls of film that thousands of people may view someday. I quickly put on my sunglasses.

Rémi continues to wave me closer to his boat—closer to that monster camera lens he holds. He adopts an obliging, almost obsequious demeanor that must work well for coaxing reluctant people like me into his photographs. Gifted and gregarious, and an excellent photographer, he's shot for many reputable publications in the West and finds himself "in demand" in the business, magazines soliciting him for his work. It had been hard to find someone willing to paddle for weeks with me in the Saharan sun who also happened to be an expert photographer (the National Geographic folk are especially picky about their photography). Not to mention that photographers' rates tend to be quite expensive—anywhere from $400 to $600 a day (writers, on the other hand, are paid only for the finished article, regardless of how many days they spend in the field). And so they solicited Rémi. He offered his services to the magazine at a bargain price, but with the concession that he be allowed to bring his girlfriend along (as his "assistant," he explained—a fairly common practice in his business), rent a large, motorized river barge, and hire three Malian men to do such things as cook meals, handle the boat, and set up the couple's tent each night.

Rémi's camera finds me now, the telephoto lens aimed at my face and clicking away as I paddle alongside his boat. I feel like some sort of B-grade movie star with Rémi as my paparazzi. Half the town of Diafarabé has gathered to see what the big deal is, and they strain their eyes as if looking for something to justify all the hullabaloo. *Just me*, I want to tell them. My face and shirt covered with sweat, my bush hat crammed on my head, my arms crispy red. I suspect they're disappointed—hell, I would be. But it is enough of a show to see a lone white woman in an inflatable kayak.

There is the usual screaming and excitement from the kids—but perhaps more so this time, with all the picture-taking. I dip my hat into the water and put it back on to cool my head. It's hot—97 degrees, according to my thermometer—and technically I've barely entered the South Sahara. I know the heat will become worse, though it already feels as bad as I'd like it to get.

Rémi's girlfriend comes over to greet me. She's a lithe, pretty redhead from the States named Heather, a graduate of the Yale theater school now living in Paris with Rémi. This is the first time, she tells me, that she's been to a place like this. A place as poor as Mali.

Yes. Poor. Mali is a place where people resell syringes and water bottles, fashion flip-flops from used car tires. I've been to other countries just as poor, places like Madagascar and Bangladesh and Nepal, so that when I see Mali all around me, a strange numbness of familiarity comes over me. A numbness that is part acceptance, but part resignation, too. Inevitably, I become filled with this strong desire to Do Something about it, which often succumbs to feelings of futility.

I look out at Diafarabé now, a collection of tightly winding streets and adobe dwellings constructed on a round peninsula that juts into the river. It looks reasonably prosperous to me, but I haven't gotten out of the boat to walk the streets.

I remember arriving in the Malian capital of Bamako on my first day. The poverty seemed to smack of truth to me: the red mud streets, the women without hands, begging for money. Donkey carts heaped with hay or rice or cooking pots, struggling to market. The very richest men cutting through it all in their slick black Mercedes Benzes, windows tinted to protect their eyes from more than just the sun. All of this, West Africa. Mali. Fourth poorest country in the world. A country that limps if it moves forward at all. The average income, $250 per family per year. If they're lucky. Or you could find yourself sleeping on the street corner in your mother's lap, like the children I saw, noses running, bellies distended. I kept passing out Malian money to the hands that reached toward me. Bills worth 50 cents, a dollar. I'd go back to the bank, get stacks of the small, crumbling confetti bills, try to pass them out to every needy person I met. I placed bills between the arm stumps of women with leprosy, and they asked me to place them in their little plastic pails instead so the local boys wouldn't rob them. Boys with the audacity to rob starving women without hands. The women apologized for the request, for inconveniencing me.

I'd stood before my dumpy hotel, looking down a street of hard-packed red clay turning slowly to mud in the drizzling rain. The air smelled alternately of rotting fruit and urine and diesel exhaust, ancient wrecks of cars groaning by, propelled by some mysterious force of human ingenuity. Women wore colorful pagnes and sat on the sides of the street, selling mangoes or bananas laid out on tarps. More prosperous vendors built themselves tiny wooden shacks, from which they sold cigarettes or writing materials or the ubiquitous Coca-Cola (always drunk on-site, the returned bottles worth more than the soda inside).

I walked for miles down dirt streets lined with great shade trees, bordered by gutters full of raw sewage. I passed old women with leprosy, missing hands and feet, begging in the dirt. There were blind women. Women suffering from AIDS with small children in their arms. Boys with legs contorted behind them by polio, rolling around the street on crude dollies. The poverty greeted me on every street corner and along every road. I quickly ran out of spare change or bills to drop in all the extended palms.

Interested in African art, I asked passersby for directions to the National Museum. Their directions led me to the edge of town, to a fenced-in area: a field of rubble.

"Is this the National Museum?" I asked a passing man.

He nodded.

"Here?"

He nodded.

I surveyed the rubble. For some reason, none of the people giving me directions mentioned that there was no actual museum to speak of. It was indicative of a country still struggling to find its footing amid the idealism and corruption of post-independence days. We needed to be content that there was a place for a museum, and rubble to represent it, for these were signs of hope. Day and night, Bamako's heat was thick and tropical, like an uncomfortable blanket wrapped around me. I returned to town.

I wandered through the *grand marché*, or city market, which extended well beyond the main cement building into a chaotic labyrinth overtaking street after street. Nearly anything could be found there, if one had the endurance to travel down the unending lanes of wares. Dealers usually specialized in a single product: ballpoint pens, safety pins, plastic bags made from fertilizer sacks, used American T-shirts printed with basketball team logos or rock stars' visages. One area, devoted exclusively to butchered meat, displayed animal parts in various stages of preparation; I watched where I walked to avoid stepping in the blood puddles. Thrifty consumers crowded around fly-covered sheep heads and cow tongues and tails— the cheapest meats—while piles of shiny offal rested like plum-colored pudding in plastic basins at the merchants' feet. It was nearing 90 degrees and there was no refrigeration, but this didn't seem to bother any of the people making purchases. Omnipresent black clouds of flies landed and flew from one piece of meat to another. Cowed dogs crept beneath tarps, stealing away scraps.

I stopped at a vendor selling bolts of colorfully printed cotton cloth, commonly used for women's pagnes and tops, and bought a couple of meters. Going next door, to where men and women sat behind foot-operated sewing machines making people's clothes, I paid an old man to make me a couple of skirts for my kayaking trip. You could order anything there, and it would be made in a matter of minutes by expert hands. I explained that I'd like elastic at the top—a preference of practicality over the wrapped sarong—and he gave a boy some money and sent him off. The boy returned out of breath, handing over rolls of elastic. My waist and leg length was quickly measured, the man sat down to his machine, and ten minutes later he handed over two skirts, hemmed and pleated. When I asked how much, he stated his price in Malian money: $1.50. He looked at me warily; I could tell he thought he had overcharged me. When I doubled the amount and handed it to him, he touched it to his forehead and smiled a toothless grin.

I decided to visit the fetish market, a taboo and sacred place on the outskirts of Bamako's main market. While most cities or towns have one, foreigners were not encouraged to visit, and people were forbidden to take photos. The two drivers I flagged down refused to drive me there. Many Malians believe these markets are places of dark magic, and not for casual viewing by foreigners or interlopers.

People went to them in order to purchase ingredients for different spells, animist traditions remaining such an integral part of West African culture that they're still practiced by many members of the Christian or Islamic faiths. Most Malians carry grigri charms full of special ingredients or prayers meant to protect them from life's myriad unfavorable circumstances. There are ways to alter nearly everything that happens—well-established spells and rituals that can effect some control over future or external events. Sick children can be saved, infertile women brought to child, businessmen blessed with riches. But the correct products must be purchased, the proper rituals performed. Witch doctors were generally consulted for such purposes, employing a number of magical methods to achieve the desired result. The more difficult and demanding the request, the greater and more expensive the ingredients or sacrifices needed for the spell. Thus, clients received a laundry list of necessary items and went shopping at the fetish market.

I spent an hour searching for the place until a friendly Indian store owner told me exactly where it was. Located on the far edge of the market, it took up a wide swath and was full of vendors with tarps laid on the ground on which were myriad dried plant concoctions and animal body parts. The air smelled putrid. Men held up rotting monkey heads, dried lizards, snake skins, waving them in my face as I walked by. Every conceivable item was represented there, from leopard paws to antelope testicles. Many of these animals couldn't be found in Mali—or even in West Africa—and had to have been imported over vast distances.

A fetish dealer called me over. He whispered something and opened a metal box. Flies rushed out into the sunlight, and I saw a live cayman and a falcon inside. The cayman was completely bound up with cord, its slat eyes leveled on mine. The bird, mouth open in thirst, shook from fear, its mahogany-colored feathers rumpled and filthy, its legs and wings tied tightly with string. I imagined buying it, setting it free. But it would be replaced by a new one. A cycle. The endless, nearly untouchable suffering.

⎯⎯⎯

HEATHER ASKS ME HOW MY TRIP'S BEEN SO FAR. "FINE," I SAY, which is what I say when I don't feel like explaining how I really feel about anything. For example, how I'm embarrassed about being photographed by Rémi right now. How when I was staying in Prague

I used to always walk several blocks out of my way to avoid being photographed by all the tourists on the Charles Street bridge.

"It's pretty damn hot," I say to her.

"Yeah, it is!" Her pale skin is flushed and beads with perspiration. Rémi tells me he's been waiting for me all morning in this heat. And as the afternoons don't provide any decent lighting, there's been nothing for him to take pictures of. Just the waiting. He says he's been reading a good book about the explorations of René Caillié.

Heather rests under the pinasse's awning, drinking bottled water and trying to escape from the sun. I look down the Niger, in the direction I have to go. The shores on either side appear dusty and parched, holding few trees. Such a long way to Timbuktu. I feel that slice of panic and horror in my gut: Why this crazy journey? I wonder what Rémi and Heather think about my trip, the idea of kayaking some 600 miles on this river, in this heat, for no reason that could ever sound logical. I'm reminded of the men of history who claimed to have climbed a mountain "because it's there," but I don't believe them for a minute. We are all at the mercy of a whole slew of forces that are more easily ignored than faced. Forces out of childhood, forces from present causes and conditions, forces as enigmatic as life itself, that tell us we must try to achieve something or get somewhere. No expedition, no journey, no personal challenge seems a product of whim or accident, initiated because something is simply "there."

I wait until the camera stops clicking, wring out my long-sleeved shirt in the waters of the Niger, and put it on in an attempt to cool off. Time to go. I bid *kambe*—goodbye—to the watching crowd, wave goodbye to Rémi and Heather and their crew. Rémi gives me instructions to wait for him at a particularly picturesque village downriver called Koa.

CHAPTER FIVE

❧

I APPROACH KOA AFTER TEN HOURS OF PADDLING, HAVING PASSED villages where everyone lined up on shore, beating on drums and yelling at me for no apparent reason. It is the first time I've experienced such hostility on my trip, and I can't account for it. I pull out my map and see that, geographically, I'm near the inland city of Djenné, conquered or controlled by various peoples throughout history—Moors, Malians, Songhai, Moroccans, French—which might explain the region's unusual suspicion toward foreigners. Djenné itself is the site of the largest mud mosque in the world, and it once competed with Timbuktu as the scholarly headquarters for Islam in West Africa. Today, it remains a very sacred place, inhabited by people who are said to be the most pious and orthodox of Mali's Muslims. Even Mungo Park strictly avoided Djenné on his first brief journey on the Niger. He wrote, "I was apprehensive that, in attempting to reach … Jenné, I should sacrifice my life to no purpose." He reported that the people of Djenné had different roots from Malians farther south, speaking a different language, and concluded that the Moorish presence there made an attempted visit too dangerous.

I see from my map that today's journey probably took me past Park's turnaround point on that first trip. He stopped "two short days' journey" from Djenné, which would place him near Koa. This means that I've officially reached Park's point of no return, and it gives me the creeps.

I recall the kindly villages I passed earlier on, full of children's waves of greeting, wondering if a mere change in geography can explain people's reactions to me. All I know is that, from now on, I'll be unable to draw any satisfying conclusions about any of the villages I pass. This is unsettling. Better they be one way or the other, better I'm able to forecast something—anything—about them during this trip. I keep looking for something substantial and permanent, something to count on, and yet I'm constantly unhinged by the sheer unpredictability of what I discover each day. I feel as if I'm paddling more and more into some kind of unknown, the heat rising each day, the sun more dazing. Mungo Park must have experienced the same thing, this world of West Africa confounding him with its lack of guarantees. And there is a certain point when you acquiesce to the discomfort of not knowing, and I'm almost there. I can feel the burnout that inevitably precedes the giving in, the end of all resistance.

The torn muscle in my arm throbs, but the other muscles seem to have compensated for it, and I find it doesn't hurt as much as before. This is a blessing I hadn't counted on, assuming it would only get worse. I was actually thinking I might have to stop this trip if it did, if the pain became too excruciating, or if my arm completely gave out. But it's as if my arm knew I wasn't going to stop, for all its complaining, and so my body did what it could to handle the problem, strengthening other muscles in place of the weakened one, healing the injury at some mysterious level.

Rémi chose to meet me at Koa mainly because of the large mud mosque close to the river. It is a photographer's dream shot, the spiky minarets casting a raw, primal beauty onto the silver spread of the Niger. A stream cuts through town, adobe homes rising on either side and connected by an arcing bridge made of palm trunks and planks of wood. During the height of the rainy season, the stream floods and the two sides of Koa are cut off from each other completely. To stare at Koa is to enter pure imagination, the wondrous worlds of childhood fancy. It's a place that seems too far, too foreign to ever breathe life outside my mind. I watch the Niger unfurling waves against the low clay shore, men striding by in long silk grand bubu robes that reach to their knees, and the women, hair plaited with gold, bend over the river in pagnes and head wrappings of such bright colors, such intensity, that my eyes suffer to take it all in.

The crowds on shore spot me as I paddle toward them, and finally something becomes familiar: the exclamations, the stares of people confounded by what they see, the rushing of women and children down to the river to get a better look. Men throw down the nets they're mending. Goats scream and run out of the way. Chickens dash for cover. It is utter mayhem, and I am the sole cause.

I smile at the people as I drag my kayak onto shore. They press in so close to me, however, that I'm unable to move anymore, and so I stand in the midst of the groping hands and loud questions, helpless. An old man comes up behind the crowd with a large stick and, incredibly, starts striking people hard on their backs. The crowd disperses immediately, and I'm afforded a small passageway through which to walk.

"Where's the chief?" I ask in Bambarra and then in French. The old man points beneath an ancient tree, which I should know by now is the best place to find any chief in Mali. I walk up to the doogootigi and greet him. Another thing that's familiar to me by now: he frowns at me. I pull out some bills for *cadeau,* a gift, and put them in his hand, asking if I can spend the night. He takes my money, counts it, smells it, and pockets it casually like some kind of Godfather. His face releases no hint of a smile. The old man with the big stick steps forward, tells me his name is Seku Mayantawa, and that he'll put me up for the night. I agree.

I grab my backpack from the kayak, and with Seku walking before me, beating away onlookers, we reach his home. It's a collection of several adobe huts forming a large courtyard. He spreads out a mat under a veranda and instructs me to sit down. Several little kids run in with my kayak balanced on their heads, and they drop it beside me. Following them is a crowd even larger than that on the shore, and the people surround me, staring and exclaiming. Some of them in the front row sit down so that the people behind them can see better. They are not, I notice, going anywhere anytime soon.

I sigh. I give some money to Seku as a gift, hoping he'll eventually run everyone out of here. One of his wives pushes through the crowd to inquire what I'd like for dinner. She offers chicken and noodles, which sound like delicacies to me. As payment, I give her a large silver coin I brought from home, and she presses it to her chest, thanking me. Another ally, I hope. More people crowd into the courtyard until there's nowhere to walk.

And now I experience another familiar, all-too-annoying problem that has become a trademark of this trip: being surrounded by an entourage of people when I have to pee. That's one thing the explorers of old never wrote about—how they managed to relieve themselves in these oddball places. The difficulties—not to mention dangers—that Sir Edmund Hillary must have experienced whipping it out on the top of Mount Everest. That sort of thing.

I sit down on my mat, looking at everyone, staring at them as they stare at me: the women's intricate cornrows, the boys' little mohawks. One boy holds a deflated soccer ball, and I convince him to hand it over to me. I take out my kayak's foot pump and blow up the ball, sealing the faulty valve with a piece of duct tape. The crowd is amazed by the pump, the tape, amazed by the bag of tricks that I have with me, and they're all barely a foot away from me now, gazing down at the soccer ball that I've just made functional. I toss the ball back to the boy, but it just bounces off his chest. He stares at me, paralyzed with surprise.

"Ça va?" I ask him, smiling.

He just looks at me, another boy grabbing the ball and running away with it.

A man pushes through the crowd to greet me. From his proud deportment and fine white shirt, I can tell he's someone important in Koa. He shakes my hand and his fingers linger in mine longer than I'd prefer. I remove my hand from his and start taking notes.

"Are you a writer?" he asks in perfect French.

"Yes," I say.

"Are you married?"

"I hope not."

"I don't understand." He leans close to me, smiling. "Are you married?"

"Not to my knowledge."

His eyes are leveled on mine. Too much intimacy in his stare. I ask Seku how many people live in Koa, hoping the other guy will go away.

"One thousand five hundred," Seku says.

"What tribe is this?"

"Bozo."

It's the first Bozo village I've stayed at, and already I'm not liking it much. I miss the Fulani villages with the cows wandering everywhere and the calabashes of warm milk, and the gentle hospitality that made me feel safe and at home. Here, with the close, gaping crowds, it feels like a madhouse. I'm experiencing exactly what Park must have 200 years ago, while staying in another large Malian village. He wrote in his narrative:

I was so completely surrounded by the gazing multitude, that I did not attempt to dismount.… [A messenger] had orders to procure me a lodging, and see that the crowd did not molest me. He conducted me into a court, at the door of which he stationed a man, with a stick in his hand, to keep off the mob, and then shewed me a large hut, in which I was to lodge. I had scarcely seated myself … when the mob entered; it was found impossible to keep them out, and I was surrounded by as many as the hut could contain. When the first party, however, had seen me, and asked a few questions, they retired, to make room for another company; and in this manner the hut was filled and emptied thirteen different times.

The guy with the white shirt is still lingering. I get up to take a walk around town, hoping I won't be treated to my own 13 visits by "the mob." If I'm lucky maybe I can find a private moment to relieve myself in the not-so-discreet mud hole behind Seku's house. I walk across the stream cutting through town, past a storefront with an Osama bin Laden picture hanging on the wall. A slice of fear cuts through me. The crowd, rather than leaving, simply follows behind me in a long stream of onlookers. It is absolutely impossible to be alone.

I return to the courtyard. Someone has spread out a foam mattress for me to sleep on, as it's too hot to sleep inside one of the buildings. I sit down on it to do some writing before Seku's wife finishes dinner, the crowd reassembling around me. I try to ignore everyone now, and people sit down nearby, whispering. The more industrious among them demand in poor French, "*Donnez-moi cinq cents francs.*" Give me 500 francs. New groups of onlookers arrive to replace the few stragglers heading home for dinner. No one does anything but watch me as if I were a particularly provocative zoo animal.

I manage to get some writing done. Night comes, and Seku brings a kerosene lamp for my use, bugs sailing against it and crashing into me. The crowd murmurs whenever I do something—pulling insect bodies from my hair, eating a chicken drumstick, turning a page of my journal. I remember visiting the zoo as a kid, and how I'd ooh and aah at the chimpanzees when they peeled a banana or picked a bug from their arm. In Koa, I'm just another hairy simian. Exhausted from all the paddling today and wanting to go to bed, I ponder ways of getting rid of the crowd that won't involve borrowing Seku's club—which seems to be the most effective form of Malian crowd dispersal to date. It's one thing to ignore everyone when I'm writing, but I know I'm not going to be able to sleep very long with nearly a hundred people gathered around me all night, listening to me snore.

I have an idea: I will set up my tent on the foam mattress. But, predictably, the tent construction only brings more people dashing into the courtyard to see the show. Fortunately, I have a small backpacking tent that sets up quickly. I make sure I put on the rain fly so no one can look inside. Climbing in, I experience the first bout of privacy I've yet had in Koa. It's incredibly hot with the rain fly on and no air flow, the 98-degree heat from the day still thick in the air. I sit and take a sweat bath, waiting for the people outside to get bored and go home. My plan works. (Poor Mungo could have used a tent like mine to save him from this.) The crowd starts to disperse, but I keep peeping outside to make sure no one is left. Finally: freedom. I creep out of the tent and run to Seku's mud hole to take my long-awaited bathroom break.

If you can sleep anywhere in a village along the Niger, the roof of an adobe house is the best place to do it. I take down my tent and sneak up clay steps to the top of Seku's house. Only Koa's mosque is higher than I am now. I spread my sleeping pad on the hard clay of the roof, the stars in a dazzling spread above me, a light breeze drying my sweat-covered clothes. I lie down and study the stars for a while, picking out Cassiopeia and Pegasus, watching the moon rising over the huts to the east. No one to bother me. No one knowing I'm here—

I hear footsteps. The man with the crisp white shirt and lingering handshake climbs up the stairwell and walks over to me.

"*Bonsoir, mademoiselle,*" he says, smiling.

"Yeah. *Bonsoir,*" I say.

"You aren't married, are you? I don't see a ring."

"Nope," I say in English. And in French: "I want to sleep now."

"Yes," he says. "Of course. Tell me, do you have a boyfriend?"

"In America," I lie.

"But he is in America and you are here."

A clever man. I prepare my bed, knowing where this conversation is headed. All I know is that I'm not in the mood.

"Do you want a Malian boyfriend?" he asks.

"I thought you'd never ask," I say.

"Miss?"

"I don't want a boyfriend. I want to sleep now." I look him in the eye; I make sure I can get up quickly, in case I have to defend myself.

"Give me your address. I will write to you."

"Tomorrow," I say. "I want to sleep now."

"Can I sleep here with you?"

I stand and point to the stairs. "Go," I say. "Leave."

"Why can't I sleep with you?"

"I'm going to hurt you," I say in English. I look over the side of the roof and see the wife I'd given the silver coin to. I call to her.

"*Ça va?*" she yells up.

But the man is already heading down the stairs like a guilty child. Down below, I watch him stride across the courtyard, his white shirt glowing in the darkness. She follows him with her eyes then looks back at me.

"*Ça va, maintenant,*" I say. Everything's fine now.

"Don't worry," she says. She closes the door of the courtyard behind him and locks it.

I lie down. The same stars greet me, but it's harder to see them. My heart beats louder in my chest.

⌒

RÉMI ARRIVES IN THE LATE MORNING. I CAN HEAR HIS BOAT LONG before I see it, the great engine chugging him down this long sweep of the Niger. It's not often that the people of Koa get visitors in one of the large river barges, so most of the town's population heads to shore to see who's coming. Me, I hide on the roof for as long as possible, to avoid the crowds.

When Rémi starts to get close to the village, I pack my things and leave my sanctuary. I walk to the river, the crowd promptly surrounding me. Kneeling down on the muddy bank, I wait, people pointing and gesticulating above me, pressing in from all sides. I'm not sure what his photo op is going to entail, and I'm ready to just leave Koa behind. I'm cranky today; I didn't sleep well last night. I kept waking, expecting the man in the white shirt to come up those stairs again to bother me. And what do Malian women do, if such a thing happens? Do they yell and kick him in the balls? Fortunately, I don't see him anywhere this morning. And anyway, Rémi's coming. Worst-case scenario, I can say the Frenchman's my boyfriend— a very jealous boyfriend with a bad temper.

I sigh and wait, and soon the large boat glides toward shore. I stand up to wave, in case Rémi can't see me in the mass of people. He's leaning off the side of the boat, camera in hand, another around his neck. The kids start up a heated chorus of "*Ça va! Ça va! Ça va!*"

"*Oui, oui. Okay. Ça va, mes enfants, ça va, ça va.*" Rémi tries to quiet them, which proves impossible. "*Bonjour, Kira,*" he says to me instead. We eye each other knowingly: a mutual understanding of what it's like to be engulfed by these crowds, to be watched by hundreds of eyes, to lose all semblance of privacy.

Rémi gets out of the boat, followed by Heather.

I walk up to her. "This place is a madhouse," I warn her.

As if on cue, Seku, my benefactor, comes striding toward shore, wearing a straw hat and holding his stick. He starts whipping any bodies that cross his path. Kids screech and run off; young men give him a wide berth. Before long he's cleared a path for us.

Rémi says he'd like to get some shots around town, pictures of me looking at things and taking down notes. Kira-the-Writer type shots. So I follow him dutifully, and he has me sit on the end of the tall palm trunk bridge with my pen and notebook. I try to look contemplative, staring off at the mosque, down at the river, at my notes. I've never done this sort of thing before, and I feel utterly ridiculous.

We head into the narrow streets for more photos. Seku follows, wielding his switch at the kids who wander into Rémi's shots. I sit at the end of long alleyways, pretending to write in my notebook, while Rémi shoots from different angles and with different lenses. I stand beside Seku in particularly photogenic locations and hold mock conversations with him while the cameras go off. An hour passes in this way. Rémi's supply of film seems endless.

Seku takes us into the big mosque for some canned shots on the roof. It's a rare privilege for a white person, a non-Muslim, to be allowed to enter a mosque in Mali, but Seku is a good guy for all his ardent switching of the kids. The mosque is bare inside but for a podium. I was expecting something akin to the ostentation of a Buddhist temple or a Christian church, but there are no paintings or gilded figures or elaborate filigree altars inside; nothing but white walls. I sit in the dim emptiness against a pillar, in a shaft of sunlight, trying to look profound for Rémi's photos. Heather, being thoughtful, runs forward to hide my bra strap. Rémi alternates between giving me rapid directions and praising the way I'm standing or holding my head, as if I were in the middle of a *Vogue* shoot. Seku stands off to one side, watching it all, uncomprehending.

It couldn't be easy being a photographer and doing this sort of thing. I give Rémi a lot of credit. Just the idea of arriving suddenly and sweeping through town with cameras in hand, before anyone realizes what's happening. Having to deal with writers like me, who find it all bizarrely absurd. Having to clear the kids away from shots, and placate village officials, and make sure you have enough spare change to pay off all the locals. Rémi has a certain deferential quality to his demeanor and speech, and he uses an interesting combination of flattery and forcefulness that gets him the shots he's known for in the magazine business; people—including me—tend to acquiesce readily to his wishes. For him to do it any other way, to be too demanding or too accommodating, would surely be detrimental to his work.

We head up to the roof of the mosque, the spiky mud minarets surrounding us like castle turrets. The Niger passes in the distance to my right; to my left, beyond the border of the town, I see only cultivated green fields. Rémi has me sit down next to Seku and hold another pretend conversation with him.

"That's right, Kira, look at him. Turn your head. Now look at me. That's great. That's perfect. Now look at him again. Talk to him." And on it goes. I look at Seku, at his old, wrinkled face.

"I'm sorry about this," I whisper to him in French.

He tells me it's all right; he is my comrade-in-the-absurd. And finally Rémi is done, has acquired all the shots he thinks he needs in Koa, and he thanks me for being a good sport. Now, he'll take photos of my departure on the Niger, and then I'll be on my own again.

I head back to the shore, some little kids with mohawks carrying my kayak back from Seku's house. I put my gear inside and get in, and Rémi has me paddle back and forth along the shore, pretending to be departing each time. I wave goodbye to the people over and over, and they play along, waving back, and at last the goodbye is for real. I find Seku in the crowd and give him a parting wave, and now it is the great Niger River again, and nothing to do but paddle. Rémi gives me the name of a hotel in Mopti, saying he'll find me there. His great boat chugs past to the northeast. I have the river all to myself again.

CHAPTER SIX

~

I PADDLE DOWN A LONELY STRETCH OF THE NIGER, PASSING THE occasional small village of thatch or adobe huts resting in heat waves. I travel in the middle of the river, hoping to preserve my distance from people on shore so that I won't create a ruckus. Sometimes I find it amazing that I'm doing this kind of trip because I'm not what some would call an "extrovert." I've always valued solitude and anonymity, yet here I do nothing but attract attention to myself at every turn. For me, it's a bigger personal challenge approaching and propositioning people in villages for a place to sleep than actually doing all the paddling to Timbuktu. Before I left, friends back home asked me if I wouldn't be "scared" traveling alone on this river, and I found it hard convincing them that I'd experience more anxiety arriving at strange villages. This trip pulls me out of my comfort zone like none other, out of a place that is usually so strongly fortified that I get reclusive.

On shore, several children shout when they see my kayak. They leave their village, running along the mud bank, yelling, beckoning. I wave to them, but I know better than to stop and risk being overrun by the crowd. Still, children are safe and artless. They always have curiosity, not ill intent. If I fear anyone, it is the adults. Men who might want to do me harm. I was warned, in particular, not to kayak alone in the vicinity of Mopti, because the city breeds malcontents, young men with boats of their own, looking to rob a "rich *tubab*." While I never forget my vulnerability on this river—it stays with me like an itch—I don't let it stop what I'm doing. I just tolerate it, adjust to it. Usually, it doesn't trouble me too much.

Until times like now.

There are four young men in a speedboat, fast approaching me. Boats with outboards are rarities on this river—this is only the second speedboat I've encountered since the beginning of my trip. Mali's utter poverty extends to its waterways, where the best most people can do is to rig sails to increase their speed. In a country with few roads, procuring enough petrol to run an outboard would preclude such a luxury for any but the wealthiest Malians living along the Niger. This is all good news for me and my safety: in my swift, lightweight kayak, I can usually outrun even the most dogged pursuer in a dugout canoe. But, when faced with the speed and maneuverability of a speedboat, I have no way whatsoever to protect myself.

I can only hope that these men don't wish me any harm. I put my can of mace in my lap and paddle as quickly as I can toward shore. As the speedboat comes to a fast stop beside me, I continue paddling to try to prevent anyone on board from grabbing hold of my kayak or the things inside. But too late—one man has seized my lead rope. He wraps it several times around his hand, pulling my kayak snug against the boat. Their outboard chugs and spits into the gray water.

"*Bonjour,*" the man says, standing over me. My mind runs over my options. They're few and abysmal. There's no escape in the middle of a river, nowhere to "run" to. I can see a village about a half mile ahead on the left-hand shore. If I have to, maybe I can convince these men to let go of my kayak so I can paddle to shore, get out, flee to the village.

"*Bonjour*," I say impatiently from behind my sunglasses, not making eye contact, waiting for their inevitable request for *l'argent*, money. All I know is that it's important not to show fear. Better impatience or anger than fear. That lesson was grilled into me during my martial arts training—to not present myself as a lesser opponent, a victim. To feel and present an attitude of strength at all times.

"Give me money, *tubab*," the man says in French. His friends extend their palms and make similar requests.

I do nothing.

"*Tubab*," he says louder, as if I haven't heard him. "*Tubab!* Give me money." He tugs on the lead rope wrapped around his hand.

I sit back, rest my elbows on the paddle, and wait. I have all the damn time in the world. I am prepared to sit here the entire afternoon if I have to. Luckily, my daypack with my money and passport is secured behind my seat today; if they wanted to take it, they'd have to physically remove me from the kayak.

The man calls to me again, and when I don't respond for the third time, he and his buddies whisper among themselves in a tribal language.

"Do you speak French?" the man suddenly asks me in French.

I give him no answer. Reaching for my water bottle, I take a long sip and then chuck it between my feet.

"Money," the man says in rough English. "*Psst, psst! Tubab!*"

The men start talking to each other again. I start to clean out the dirt from beneath my fingernails.

"Money," the man says to me. He yanks at the lead rope, trying to get my attention. "*Tubab! Cadeau!*"

The children from the village I passed, who had been running along the shore all this time trying to keep up with my kayak, appear on the nearby bank. When they call out to me, I get a sudden idea: I vigorously beckon them with my hand. The crowd of boys exchange glances, and, hesitating for just a moment, dive eagerly into the river. Accomplished swimmers, they race each other to my kayak. When they reach me, out of breath, they grab hold of the side of my boat. They smile broadly at me as if in victory.

"*Ca va! Ca va!*" they yell to me.

"*Ca va!*" I yell in return.

My kayak isn't big enough to support all of them, so they start trying to climb into the speedboat. The men angrily order them out, but they've made it a game trying to get inside, and their little bodies start springing over the sides. The man in charge of the outboard revs it and starts to move the boat forward, but this doesn't deter the invaders. After more angry yells to them, he orders the release of my kayak and cranks the motor to full throttle. In an instant, the boat surges forward. Boys leap over the side, treading water as they watch the boat roar away down the river. Relieved, I pass out chunks of dried apricot to my saviors. We suck on the fruit together, smiling at each other, floating along with the Niger.

I never know how I'll handle these kinds of threatening situations until they arise. Yet, as a woman traveling alone, I know they're as inevitable as the changing weather along the Niger. The truth: my gender will always make me appear more vulnerable. But to not travel anywhere out of fear, or to remain immobilized in a state of hypervigilance when I do, feels akin to psychological bondage. I do not want to give away that kind of power.

THE NIGER CHURNS AND SHIFTS IN A STRONG WIND. I PADDLE AGAINST the gales, barely creeping forward, hitting currents that propel me around bends and throw me into high waves. But there are no storms, at least. No rain. Just gray skies, and the unrelenting river that mocks all sense of progress. I pull over to a sandbar to rest and eat a Snickers.

I've developed a steady speed to my paddling that I can maintain for a couple of hours without stopping, my arm and upper-body muscles looking more well-defined than they've ever been. After overcoming the psychological protests to beginning a day of paddling, my body settles into the routine of the up and down strokes. My stamina has greatly increased, as when I used to train every day as a runner, and for the first time during this trip, kayaking feels like a natural expression of my body, an extension of myself.

I've been hoping to reach Mopti today, and so of course the river and weather aren't cooperating with me. It seems more than mere coincidence that as soon as I want to get somewhere, all forces seem to marshal themselves toward preventing me. I think I can understand why the locals believe in a god of the river; why, when eating on the Niger, they drop a portion of their meal into the water as an offering. When you do the paddling yourself, when there's no outboard on your boat to do the work, when you must depend exclusively on the natural environment and your physical abilities to get anywhere, the Niger becomes more than a waterway—it becomes a personality. I understand implicitly what is meant by "becoming one with nature" as soon as I'm obliged to rely on forces out of my control. And this is perhaps the strangest revelation about my journey to date, and the oddest transformation that I see occurring within me: I feel caught in a relationship with these waters. The paddling has become personal; the Niger has turned into a fickle parent making constant demands of me and thwarting all my plans.

Mopti represents my journey's halfway point, and my mind, hopelessly spoiled by First World luxuries, craves what I'll be able to find there. Hot showers, filling meals, flea-free beds. When I've asked fishermen how far away Mopti is, they never reply in terms of kilometers. Such a distance analysis is worthless when you're doing the paddling yourself and must face conditions that can't be predicted. Instead, invariably, they stare up at the sun and reply in terms of paddling hours. Ten hours, maybe. Or twelve hours, if there's a bad storm. Eight, possibly, but only with an agreeable river and fast paddling.

I get in my kayak again and paddle as fast as I ever have, but none of it is enough to get me anywhere near Mopti. The sun starts to set, and I circle bend after bend, straining my eyes for sight of a distant radio tower—the harbinger of all big towns along the river. The impatience and annoyance I'm feeling is reaching epic heights. But I see nothing, and I must just let go, resign myself to the fact that I won't reach Mopti or any of its comforts tonight.

I pass a single domed hut on the mud shore, constructed entirely from woven thatch mats. A man stands beside it and yells out to me in excellent French.

"Where are you going?" he asks.

"To Mopti," I yell. And in my impatience, I again ask the familiar question: "How far is it?"

He looks at the position of the setting sun. "You'll get there at one in the morning," he says with finality. It is the finality of a man who knows the river well, and I believe him. I see the futility of continuing.

"You're welcome to spend the night with me and my family," he says. He's smiling and nodding graciously at me. His little children join him, staring at me, fingers in their mouths. I take up his offer, paddling back against the current and pulling up on the mud bank next to his canoe.

His name is Blabasy Tapoo, and it turns out that he's a Somono man. The Somono are the Niger's great fishermen, rumored to be the modern descendents of Nile River fishermen who emigrated across the Sahara in previous millennia. Mungo Park frequently wrote about the Somono—they were the ones he always entrusted with burying his dead. He also noted in his narrative the excellent fishing skills of a people who, given their techniques, were more than likely Somono: "The fisherman paddled his canoe to the bank ... stripped off his clothes, and dived for such a length of time, that I thought he had actually drowned himself, and was surprised to see his wife behave with so much indifference upon the occasion; but my fears were over when he raised up his head astern of the canoe, and called for a rope.... At length, [he] brought up a large basket, about ten feet in diameter, containing two fine fish." I see similar large baskets in Blabasy's canoe, each handmade with strips of wood and cord. The traditions have barely changed over the centuries.

Blabasy ties up my kayak and takes me inside his little compound. He lives in an area about 20-by-20 feet, surrounded by a thatch fence. Chickens roam about, pecking at scraps and racing from approaching children. A huge pile of firewood fills up nearly half the available space, with fish nets and underwater baskets lying on top. The straightforward simplicity of this life is obvious in the clay pots that hold millet and rice, the rolls of woven thatch building material, the small oblong hut just big enough for the family to fit inside. Clay from the riverbank has been ingeniously molded into a large oven for cooking. There is no sign of Western goods. No *need* for Western goods. All of the basics have been met. Everyone looks content and satisfied. If they need to relieve themselves, they walk off into the countryside. If they need to bathe, they have the Niger just a few feet away.

I give Blabasy a gift of some money, and he looks down at the bills with shy surprise: he wasn't expecting anything in return for his generosity. I meet Blabasy's two wives: an older woman named Niami and a girl who looks to be barely sixteen, whom at first I took to be Blabasy's daughter. But they marry young out here. Unlike the tattooed and decked-out Fulani women I've seen, these Somono women are unadorned but for small gold hoops in each ear. Both nurse babies; Blabasy tells me that he's the proud father of seven children, the two oldest with his sister in nearby Asawana village. He seems to be a good husband and dad, speaking kindly to his wives and bringing out a young daughter to bounce on his knee. I'm not surprised by the fact that he has more than one wife—it's the norm in Mali. According to Islamic law, each man is allowed a maximum of four wives, assuming he can provide for them; in the villages I've visited so far, two seems to be the going number.

As Blabasy is so unusually friendly and forthcoming, and as his great French enhances my ability to communicate with him, I want to ask him about having two wives. I'd rather ask the women themselves, but, as is the case throughout Mali, they are uneducated and have no knowledge of French whatsoever.

"Do you like having two wives?" I ask Blabasy. A stupid question, but I want to see what he says.

He speaks in a quick, stuttering, enthusiastic sort of way. He seems delighted and flattered to be answering my questions, and I'm a bit taken aback by his candor. "When one wife is pregnant," he says, "I can lie with the other." He points to the younger woman. "When neither is pregnant, I take turns. One night with her, one night with her." He smiles grandly. "I like it a lot."

"Do they get jealous?" I ask.

"No, no. I'm good to them both."

I'm wondering what the women think of the arrangement, but they do look happy together, sharing the cooking, chatting to each other.

Blabasy orders the kids to catch a couple of chickens for our dinner, and his two young boys come back, each with a screeching bird in hand. Blabasy politely excuses himself to chop off the heads. He returns a minute later, passing the twitching bodies to the women. Picking up his little girl, he bounces her on a knee and baby-talks to her. He seems to have accepted the job of babysitting the kids while his wives cook.

"Do you want more wives?" I ask him.

He grins. "Yes. But I must wait until I catch more fish during the rainy season, when I'll be rich again."

He explains to me that he lives in this lone hut on the riverbank because it's more convenient for his fishing. By setting up temporary camp here, instead of in Asawana village, which is inland, he can more easily catch and sell his fish. But it's the slow season now, as the rains have only just started, and the big fish harvests won't come until a few months from now. "In December I'll be a rich man," he says.

"What will you do until then?" I ask.

"I'll catch one or two fish a day and do nothing." He laughs and lies back, pulling his giggling children on top of him. His wives stop plucking chicken feathers and glance over at him, smiling. Blabasy, I see, is quite the family man.

We eat a big, filling dinner of chicken and rice. To top it off, Blabasy's sister brings over a calabash of freshly squeezed cow's milk from Asawana village. I notice that the family eats every part of the chicken, tendons, skin and all, spitting out the bones into a bowl. I try to follow their example, aware that I'm used to being finicky and wasteful when I eat chicken back home. Here, killing a chicken is only done on special occasions, for the arrival of an honored guest. It is a luxury.

I'm grateful I never made it to Mopti, as being with this family is a delight. I could have never predicted such a treat when Blabasy called to me from his lone thatch hut on the mud bank. It's quite a contrast to my unpleasant experience in Koa the other evening.

Blabasy turns on his tiny transistor radio and West African music floods the night. He pulls out his own foam mattress for me to sleep on, and none of my protestations will convince him to keep it for himself. I sit beside him and his kids, and we all look down the slope at the Niger flowing past in the silver moonlight. The waves make a slurping, *slap-slap* sound on the mud bank below, stars blazing above. His wives sit down by the hut, nursing their babies and staring at the opposite shore that makes only the faintest imprint in the darkness. The transistor radio drones on weakly, trying to be heard in all this immensity.

∽

SUNRISE IS ONE OF THE BEST TIMES TO PADDLE IN WEST AFRICA. IT'S before the midday heat, before most villagers wake up. Wildlife revels at this time of the morning. Four-foot-long monitor lizards crawl from the water and creep behind brush. Fish pluck at insects on the water's surface. And birds—thousands of them—fly in unbroken, undulating clouds that dip and shoot across the river. These flocks are expertly formed, not a single bird out of place, all flying with careful yet carefree precision. A cloud of them flies overhead now—that is the only word for it, a cloud—and they curl and bend in the shape of a gigantic snake, completely blocking out the sun and causing a shadow to fall over me. I stop paddling and raise my eyes to the extraordinary cacophony above. I watch the individual birds, gliding in synch with the rest of the group, no one straggling, no one breaking away. The cloud swoops toward a tree and lands all at once, the branches filled with fluttering bodies, becoming instantly alive with song. I feel the futility of trying to take in the beauty of such a scene, and so I just gape for a while, a child again.

I paddle on through the morning, not seeing a single person in a canoe to break the long spread of river before me. Perhaps this is because a storm is starting to rise, so I paddle hard, wanting to make as much distance as possible toward Mopti before it comes. Storms tend to appear from the northwest, spending hours taking over the sky with a looming darkness. I like to play guessing games with them, wondering if they'll hit me with rain or miss me altogether. Sometimes the distant thunderheads shoot out sparks of lightning, as if making threats. Other times they lose their nerve and drift overhead silently, sullenly, a light patter of rain hitting me in short-lived protest before moving on.

This time, though, I can tell it's going to be different. A great wind is already acting as harbinger for a big act to come, blowing directly against me, slowing my paddling to a crawl. Dark clouds boom and rattle, while great Saharan winds churn up the red clay soil and paint blood trails across the sky. I'm stuck in the middle of the river and rush toward shore. The winds are getting even worse, the river sloshing with three-foot-high whitecaps. It is the Jekyll-Hyde phenomenon of the Niger, the river utterly calm one moment only to burst into waves and rapids the next. And here I am caught in the capriciousness yet again, struggling with my bad arm to nose the kayak into the waves and get across before the worst of the storm hits.

I lean forward to secure my bags, and a wave broadsides my boat and flips it over. I fall out and swim to the surface, seeing my kayak bottom up and speeding steadily away. I dive for it and grab its tail, turning it over and retrieving my paddle, only to see my little backpack—the one with passport, money, journal—starting to sink nearby.

It is as if the worst of my fears are being realized, one after the other, but by treading water and holding on to the kayak, I'm able to retrieve the backpack. Pulling myself inside the boat, I fumble to get oriented in the midst of the waves and paddle toward shore with all my strength. Thunder bellows, lightning flashes. I make it to the bank, rain shooting from the sky with such force that the drops sting my skin. I huddle, shaking from adrenaline, and take a tally of what I lost: both water bottles and some packets of dried fruit, but, mercifully, nothing else. The Niger has won my submission.

I SEE A RADIO TOWER IN THE DISTANCE. THANK GOD: MOPTI. MY halfway point. It will be a dubious victory, though, with everything I own completely soaked from my kayak wipeout, and myself not quite recovered from it. Physically, I'm wasted. Mentally, I have a new and formidable respect for the wrath of the Niger. I've never wanted to get somewhere so badly—except, maybe, to Timbuktu. I've been battling impatience again, my stomach rumbling from hunger, my arms aching after a long day of paddling. In these circumstances, Mopti feels like a bastion of air-conditioning, agreeable meals, and, most of all, rooms with doors that lock: things I've grudgingly done without.

My journey on the river is inevitably teaching me humility. I am learning that the body can survive on basic foods, and that they needn't taste or look good to perform their task of quieting the stomach and providing nourishment. Even the smallest things that I take for granted in the West are nearly impossible-to-find luxuries along the Niger— lavatories, telephones, a private place to bathe. After a while of this "doing without," I start to trade the world back home for this one. I start to see, with glaring clarity, how little I actually do need, and how strongly the West tries to convince me otherwise. All those commercials back home, all those advertisements for designer clothes, scented toilet paper, Home Shopping Club miscellany. We're taught to think we need certain things if we are to be comfortable, safe, happy. And so it's all about fear. Fear of having the "wrong" rather than the "right" things, fear of not having as much as the next guy, fear of what we look like or how we sound. The endless fears. And yet, if I'm honest with myself, I see that I've been carrying in my little kayak all that I truly need: food, water, a couple of changes of clothes, medicine, a tent for shelter. The few luxuries I do have are superfluous, and they will remain buried deep in my backpack to be unearthed when I eventually head back home. The digital tape recorder. The CD player. The Faulkner novel. No use for any of those things here.

Mopti looks sizable as I approach it, large villages lining the banks of the Niger on both sides, people screaming at me to paddle over to them and give them *cadeaux*. I cut across the Niger toward the central part of town. Most boats head to the main dock, where scores of people gather to sell their wares along the river's shore. There are the enormous slabs of grayish Saharan salt. Mangoes, bananas, fried rice cakes, kola nuts. Pots and pans, flip-flops, writing supplies. Each merchant has his specialty. Every conceivable thing is represented.

I decide to avoid the crowds of the docks by stopping to the north of town. I land my kayak near a group of women washing clothes in the river, their feet submerged in a thick brown mud that smells strongly of human refuse and animal dung. Littering the shore is the typical detritus of cities—snack wrappers, broken bottles, discarded shoes. I pull my kayak out of the muck and stand on solid ground, taking a deep breath. Mopti. Finally. It seems miraculous to be here. Distant Timbuktu feels not so distant anymore.

I deflate my kayak for the first time since leaving Old Ségou. It shrinks into a simple piece of rubber. This rubber has, amazingly, kept me afloat through storms and heat and crowds, getting me and my things as far as Mopti. I can barely believe it.

Kids surround me, standing so close that I constantly have to say *pardon* in order to move. I fold up the kayak and put it in its bag, smelly mud covering my arms and dirtying my backpack and paddle. I try to rinse off in the Niger, but my feet just sink into muck up to my shins. I'm supposed to get a room at the Kananga Hotel in order to meet Rémi, so I hoist my bags to my shoulders and carry them to a nearby road to get a taxi. I wait for a while, only to look up and see the hotel sitting across the street from me. Like serendipity.

It turns out that the Kananga is Mopti's only luxury hotel. As I enter the lobby, a French couple, sitting in rattan chairs and sipping cocktails, looks at me with surprise and derision. I squeeze my bags through the main door, leaving mud smears on the plate glass. I can't imagine what I look like. I've come to forget all notions of personal appearance by now, accepting the omnipresent mud on me, the dirty sandals, the wet skirt, the sweaty T-shirt. This is simply the way things are when you've been kayaking on the Niger for a while.

French families leaving the dining room frown at me, their blond-haired children gaping and pointing. If there's one thing I'm used to by now, it's being gaped at. Fortunately, the Malian concierge doesn't seem fazed by what I look like. She smiles at me in the same way she smiles at the other guests, and there's nothing disingenuous about her expression of goodwill; she knows—as I do—that this posh hotel is just one, albeit comfortable, version of the world. I do catch her look of surprise when I open my muddy backpack to pull out a huge wad of damp Malian cash, courtesy of the National Geographic Society. I feel like some kind of illegal arms dealer. The French couple nearby notices this, too: the incongruity of a grubby woman emerging from the river, mud-smeared and greasy-haired, having a huge roll of bills. I promptly get a room. And a hot shower. I plan to sleep as if I had no intention of waking.

CHAPTER SEVEN

⤳

The hotel staff recommend to me a local man named Assou, a well-respected friend of the Peace Corps folk in town who knows about conditions along the Niger from Mopti to Timbuktu. He enters the hotel lobby, sporting a loudly patterned red silk shirt and sunglasses. We shake hands and the sunglasses come off, and I see a man with sensitive, intelligent eyes and shyness in his expression. There is also a precocious air about him, exhibited in his uncanny ability to speak English. Though he's only 28, he speaks the best, most colloquial English I've yet heard in Mali, and he knows German, French, Spanish—even a little Japanese. He is also a prodigious talker, the simplest question from me eliciting a 20-minute response.

We sit down for a while—for him to talk, me to listen. He tells me that his greatest claim to fame is having been a guide for Tom Robbins, who vacationed in West Africa, and he begins to tell me much more about the author than I ever wanted to know, everything from how Robbins visited a particular Dogon tribe to his penchant for hard-boiled eggs.

"He is a very famous American writer," Assou declares, at the end of what has become a half-hour tale. "Am I right?"

"Sort of," I say.

"He sent me a letter. It's true. I'll show it to you." He wants to get a taxi so he can show me the letter right now, back in his office. It's that important to him, proving his affiliation and friendship with Robbins. I promise him I'll see the letter later. If I remember. When I mention my trip down the Niger and what it's been like so far, Assou says I obviously didn't know about the genies that inhabit the river—every Malian knows about them—which explains why I've been having problems. It's not uncommon, he says, for people to simply disappear when traveling on the river. Even the most experienced boatmen have been known to vanish, with no trace of their bodies, the genies taking them. Genies, themselves, live in the eddies and rapids. They control the wind and current, and they alone decide whether they'll let a person pass. He says it's essential that I enlist these spirits to my cause of reaching Timbuktu, or who knows what tragedies might befall me.

At his urging, I agree to meet with him this evening to see a sorcerer for a consultation about my trip. Such consultations with sorcerers and witches are routine for most West Africans, Muslim or not. Fetishism and superstition are as alive and well in the 21st century as they were during Park's time, nearly everyone wearing *saphies*, or magic charms, meant to ward off evil and ensure success in myriad endeavors. Park could not help remarking on the charms: "These saphies are prayers or rather sentences, from the Koran, which the Mahomedan priests write on scraps of paper and sell to the simple natives, who consider them to possess extraordinary virtues.... I did not meet with a man who was not fully persuaded of the powerful efficacy of these amulets." The Koranic verses are sewn inside little leather pouches, made by special saphie-makers, and there is such a demand for encasing the verses that these craftsmen have made a good living for centuries. Assou, an avowed agnostic, still trusts his luck to the saphie that he hides beneath his shirt. He shows it to me with a smile of embarrassment, shrugging. Better not to take any chances.

Fetishism, itself, is another part of West African culture that hasn't changed much since Park's time, and Assou admits that he fears those who practice it. Every large town has its own fetish market, and Mopti is no exception. People in Mali widely believe that sacrificing live animals, or otherwise making ritual use of some part of one, be it the fur, skin, teeth, or bones, has magical utility. The fetish object is brought to a local witch doctor, who then performs a spell for the client. Invoking the powers of a dead chameleon might bring fortune for a child. Sacrificing a goat might bring success in business. But animals aren't the only victims; occasionally, people are murdered for the purposes of voodoo. Women have been found dead on the streets of Mopti with their breasts removed for special spells. Would-be politicians, wanting a guarantee that they'll win an election, have arranged for the sacrifice of albino men or women. This latter fact sounded incredible to me until Assou introduced me to the music of Salif Keita, one of West Africa's most celebrated musicians, who also happened to be an albino. Keita, who was rejected by his superstitious father (albinos are often associated with malign spirits), found himself living on the streets of Bamako. He wrote songs about his predicament there, which included being hunted by men needing albinos to sacrifice. Apparently, it had gotten so bad during the national elections that he had no choice but to flee Mali.

I leave Assou to check out Mopti for a while. It's the most comfortable place I've experienced in this country, with plenty of amenities at convenient distances from each other. There are a couple of Arab-run clothing stores offering Internet access. A pastry shop sells frosted cake tasting remarkably close to the real thing. The large tourist market beats out Bamako's and is filled with an impressive array of exorbitantly priced old African trade beads. There is also the kitsch of all touristy places in Africa: zebra-skin sandals and wallets, cowhide drums, cheap antelope carvings darkened with shoe polish. Every once in a while some more interesting items emerge: silver Tuareg Koran-holders, Dogon amulets, old brass sculptures. Tribal masks are omnipresent, with about eight prototypical designs found in most of the stalls. This selection satisfies the majority of tourists, though there will be the occasional connoisseur trying to find "a real antique." They do better looking in African art galleries back home; the best Malian merchants can do is sell them 30-year-old ones along with the dubious promise that they were "actually used."

I learn not to touch or gaze at anything for too long in these stalls, as hawkers will follow me halfway across Mopti as soon as I show even mild interest in something. They become incensed and impatient when I tell them that I have very little money to part with. I don't bother to explain that, by U.S. government standards, I've lived below the poverty level for much of my adult life as a graduate student, surviving on a trifle from teaching and magazine writing (not to mention selling my platelets). These dealers have cars much nicer than my 14-year-old Toyota Corolla, own vast quantities of rare trade beads, live in large houses filled with Western goods. But the minute I say I'm American, it's as if a transformation has occurred before their eyes, and I become some kind of Rich Foreigner with endless supplies of cash. There is nothing I can say that will modify this image they have of me; it's utterly pointless to argue with them.

I decide to look up Peace Corps Baba to see one of the best African art collections in Mali. His real name is Oumar Cisse, but Moptians coined his new name due to his close relations with the Peace Corps folk in town. Baba is something of a Malian celebrity: the Lonely Planet *West Africa* guide gives him top billing, and he sold an antique Dogon door to none other than Henry Louis Gates, Jr., who came to Mali on his *Wonders of the African World* tour a few years ago. All the taxi drivers know of "Peace Corps Baba" by name, and apparently no trip to Mopti is complete without paying him a visit.

I stop by Peace Corps Baba's home. I find him in the middle of treating an older French couple and their teenage daughter to a lavish meal on the roof of his two-story building. Baba invites me to join them. The French daughter, I notice, looks on the verge of vomiting. She holds her stomach and lets out feeble complaints about the spices in a dish, while Baba ignores her completely and brags to us about all the places he's seen in Europe. He's one of Mali's biggest exporters of African trade beads, and they've made him rich. He now spends most of his time traveling all over the world to gem and bead shows. He tells me that he goes to America only during the summer because he can't abide cold weather; he absolutely refuses to get anywhere near snow. He clutches himself and shakes his head.

"You could buy a coat," I suggest. "Maybe an Arctic parka."

He starts talking about Big Macs and fat women, and I excuse myself to head back to town. I'll look at his art some other time.

⌇

I WANDER ALONG MOPTI'S RIVERFRONT. I'M GRATEFUL THAT I'M NOT on the Niger today as I'd be battling my way through heavy wind and waves. Not to mention that Mopti provides a nice, comfortable break that I'd like to extend for a while. The city is prosperous, with 40,000 people spread out over a mile along the Niger and expanding inland into the savanna. The French built Mopti to its present bustling state, and it's full of colonial-era whitewashed cement buildings, paved but potholed streets, and a healthy Peace Corps population teaching, among other things, hand-washing. Mopti has also become the headquarters for many of Mali's most successful travel agencies and touring companies—which might explain why I can't walk even a few feet without being assailed by a guide trying to book me for a tour. Apparently there are pottery villages, colorful tribes, breathtaking scenery, all awaiting me. And how about a boat tour on the Niger?

"I do not," I tell the young man who suggested this last choice, "need a boat tour on the Niger."

But the fact that I have spoken at all is taken as encouragement, and he joins me at my restaurant table as I order fish and chips. My meal promptly arrives, and I dip a French fry in some ketchup, giving terse answers to his litany of questions—the same tedious questions that precede all Mopti tour pitches. What's my name? Where am I from? How long in Mali?

"Look," I say, sighing, "can we just get to the point?"

"I have an all-day boat tour for you," he says in poor English. "You take a boat, see the Niger. The Niger is very nice."

"You may not believe this," I say, "but I've already seen the Niger."

"You will go in my company's pinasse," he says. "It's very comfortable. It's a nice boat."

"I already have my own boat."

"No! How is this possible?"

I shrug. "I brought it from home. It's in my hotel room."

"In Africa, it's not good to tell lies," he says.

"I'm not lying. It's a red inflatable boat, and it's in my hotel room."

He stands up. He's actually getting angry with me. "I want to help you. That's all. I want you to have a nice boat tour. And what you do? You tell me lies. Do you know? The Niger is a very beautiful river."

"I'm sure it is," I tell him.

⌣

No trip to Mali is complete without seeing its most famous tourist attraction after Timbuktu: the Great Mosque in the city of Djenné. A UNESCO World Heritage site, it also has the distinction of being the largest mud building in the world. Djenné is about 90 miles southwest of Mopti, on its own little island in the Bani River. I decide to get there by *taxi brousse*, the most popular and cheapest means of travel in Mali. These vehicles are nothing more than small, ancient Toyota trucks with wooden benches in back covered by a metal frame and tarp. Hundreds of them converge on the outskirts of town in a large dirt parking area. Always on the alert, would-be passengers surround the first empty trucks that pull in. When the drivers announce their destinations, the crowds overrun the vehicles and rush to get inside, creating a shoving, crashing stampede of bodies.

I arrive early in the morning in order to have a better chance of claiming a choice corner bench spot for myself. My strategy works. People soon start to fill in after me. The taxi brousse doesn't leave until it's "full," though what constitutes "full" is a matter of individual opinion. Drivers will squeeze in as many human bodies as can be fitted inside, barring suffocation. I try as best I can to stake out my bench territory, creating a vice with my thighs and mounting a full-body resistance to the seizure of my precious space, but this proves futile. Before long, my right thigh is sitting on someone else's, my feet are in some woman's lap, and a baby is perched on my shoulders. For a truck bed that couldn't be larger than six feet by five feet, I count an extraordinary 32 bodies inside, not including the two guys hanging out the back.

At last, after an hour of cramming and crowding, the truck is ready to leave. That it can move at all is a miracle, but it finally groans out of the parking lot, shudders, and gains momentum on the road, flying along at breakneck speed. I try not to imagine an all-too-common scenario in this country: our sardine-packed taxi brousse taking a bend too quickly, overturning, and reducing the truck and its occupants to a pile of twisted metal and hamburger meat.

Across the aisle are two Belgian backpackers; the woman sits awkwardly on her boyfriend's lap, her feet dangling in the face of a small boy crouched on the floor.

"What brings you to Mali?" she asks me from behind several heads.

"I'm going to be writing an article."

"So this is your *job*?" the boyfriend says incredulously.

I extract a hand to wipe the sweat from my eyes. "Yeah," I say.

"I don't think I want your job," the woman says, frowning.

It takes us an incredible six hours to travel the 90 miles to Djenné, our truck finally stopping beside the Bani River with Djenné resting on an island before us. Accounting for our long delay were numerous stops to load and off-load passengers, which meant the tedious packing and repacking of bodies inside. We're all ordered out so the driver can make it across a muddy tract to the ferry. We try not to step on any limbs as we carefully extract ourselves. I long ago lost all feeling in my legs, and I immediately start up a dance to restore circulation. I'm particularly grateful that the baby on my shoulders has been removed. Just after we left Mopti it had gone to the bathroom, and its mother had been unable to attend to it until now. The result had been a miserable child and a dirty diaper congealing for hours in the Saharan heat. Everyone inside the truck had had to endure the inescapable, pungent shit smell.

After all this, Djenné had better be good. All I know is that I'll pay whatever it costs to charter a car back to Mopti.

We wait another hour for the ferry, the clouds unleashing a downpour that turns everything underfoot to deep mud. At last the ferry arrives and we get on, crossing the Bani River. We crowd back into the truck for the final ride into town—but not before the Belgians and I, being tubabs, are charged an exorbitant fee to enter the city. The fee reminds me of how, for hundreds of years (including the time when Park was here), foreigners were charged a duty to travel through each part of the country, and were completely barred entry into Djenné. Only Westerners in disguise had the chance of viewing the city and its mosque, as it was considered a holy Islamic city and off-limits to non-Muslims.

Djenné has been around for centuries; it was founded as early as A.D. 800 and is the oldest known city in sub-Saharan Africa. For a long time Djenné had been as important as Timbuktu, sitting at the crossroads of all the major Saharan trade routes. Gold, salt, and ivory passed through its gates, not to mention one of its most prized and lucrative commodities: slaves. Even today, there are families in Djenné who tacitly own slaves, passed down to them from the previous generation. But what makes Djenné unique is its anachronistic charm: little has changed in this town for hundreds of years. Goatherds chase their flocks down narrow alleyways lined with ancient, double-floored adobe-brick houses. Fulani women, their mouths tattooed dark blue and a gold band placed through the septum of their noses, stroll quietly through town. The focal point of everything is the Great Mosque, its three spiky mud turrets reaching above the skyline and topped with ostrich eggs (symbols of fertility and chastity). It's an enormous structure built on a platform of adobe bricks and covering an area that must be the size of an entire football field. I walk around its base, admiring the sheer breadth and elegance of its construction. Every year,

African Muslims make a pilgrimage here to pray within the mosque's walls or to study in the surrounding *madrasahs*, or Koranic schools. It's the next best thing to Mecca.

While the Great Mosque at its current size was completed in 1907, it replaced another that was originally built in the 13th century by Djenné's first Muslim ruler, the sultan Koy Konboro. I walk up to the adobe walls and run a hand over them. Their two-foot thickness supports the building's bulky weight and provides insulation from the sun's heat. Each year, torrential rains collude to wash away portions of the mosque's walls; each spring, everyone in town gathers together to replaster the outside with mud, occasioning a great local festival.

I'm not able to go inside because non-Muslims have been banned from entering since 1996. People have given me several different reasons for this, but the story I've pieced together tells of a European fashion photographer taking pictures of bikini models inside. Some Djenné residents suggest it went further than that, however, and that a porn movie was actually made; others mention only that foreigners filmed the inside without permission. Regardless, a large sign rests before the mosque, explaining that non-Muslims are *interdit* from entering.

I sit in the market area, eating a mango and trying to imagine this city as it would have been back in Park's time. Undoubtedly, aside from the upgrade of the mosque in 1907, the town would have looked nearly the same. Park, himself, had wanted to come here but finally deemed it too dangerous. The fact that the city was controlled by Moroccan kings and had a large population of Moors convinced him to give up his first river trip and return to England in 1797. Even the idea of passing the Bani River's confluence at present-day Mopti made him nervous, as Djenné and the Niger were linked by waterways. Park had valid reason for his trepidation: he'd just barely escaped with his life from brutal imprisonment with the Moors in the Sahara; his journal was riddled with references to the terror he felt at the prospect of being recaptured:

> "I had but little hope," he wrote, "of subsisting by char-
> ity in a country where the Moors have such influence.
> But above all, I perceived that I was advancing, more and
> more, within the power of those merciless fanatics;
> and from my reception both at Sego and Sansanding,
> I was apprehensive that, in attempting to even reach
> Djenné (unless under the protection of some man of
> consequence amongst them, which I had no means of
> obtaining), I should sacrifice my life to no purpose; for
> my discoveries would perish with me.... I saw inevitable
> destruction in attempting to proceed to the eastward."

BACK IN MOPTI, I MEET ASSOU SO WE CAN VISIT HIS SORCERER OF choice, a man named Salla, who will supposedly be able to tell me how to appease the genies of the Niger and reach Timbuktu. With divination and voodoo such an integral part of West African society, I'm infinitely curious to find out what it is about fortune-tellers and their spells that makes them such an indispensable part of Malian life.

I walk with Assou down a muddy alleyway in downtown Mopti. We enter a courtyard, crossing a dark room lit only by a television set. Salla's extended family lounges on foam mattresses spread on the floor, and they barely glance at us as we enter, their eyes fixed on the television screen, on an African music video. We pass by without a word, ascending old, winding adobe stairs to the second floor. Salla is in a back room, asleep, and Assou nudges him awake with his foot. He sits up, scratching his chest through his stained grand bubu robe, and straightens the white skullcap on his head. He lights a kerosene lamp in the dim room and invites us to sit on a carpet on the floor.

I don't know what I expected a sorcerer to look like. Maybe some old, wizened man with a silver beard and some sort of magical implement he waves around. Salla is the first sorcerer I've ever met, and I'm not particularly impressed. He rubs the sleep from his eyes, yawns, and mumbles wearily to Assou.

"He needs money," Assou explains to me

"Right." I place some bills in Salla's extended hand. The man's countenance brightens and he speaks.

"He needs your name," Assou says.

I tell him, and he writes down characters in Arabic to fit the pronunciation. Assou tells me that Salla will be making what is called a *turaboo beradela* in Bambarra—a consultation using both cowry shells and the Koran, illustrative of a confluence of animist and Islamic traditions. This technique—one of numerous varieties of divination available in West Africa—uses a kind of automatic writing technique to read the future and obtain answers to questions. Salla throws the shells into a shallow basket, studies them, then crouches over a notebook and begins writing furiously in Arabic.

"He didn't ask me what I wanted to know," I whisper to Assou.

"We don't need to tell him. He knows your questions when he writes your name."

"You're sure about this?"

Assou rolls his eyes at me. "Of course. This man is the best sorcerer in Mopti."

In the car coming over here, Assou had been especially cocky about Salla's abilities, so I say nothing now and watch and wait. The Arabic writing increases in speed, until Salla reaches a frenzy of impassioned scribbling. At last he stops, dropping the pen with dramatic finality and looking up at me with pursed lips. Assou has enormous respect for Salla, maintaining that he has correctly read his future each and every time he's come in for a consultation—which is now up to three times a week. Based on all of Assou's praise, I have great expectations for this man.

"Your name, 'Kira,' is interesting," Salla says, Assou translating his tribal language. "In Bambarra, it means 'prophet.' You will sit on the power chair and have a long life."

I'm starting to like this consultation.

"I have seen that you have something in mind about a man," Salla adds, staring at the Arabic scribbles, "but that might not work."

"I don't know what he means," I say to Assou.

"What you have in mind about this man," Salla emphasizes, "could come to trouble."

"But I don't *have* anything in my mind about a man."

Salla continues solemnly: "You will have four children in the future."

"Never, ever, never," I tell him.

Piqued, Salla replies in French, "I am never wrong, miss." He glares at me and looks to Assou for guidance. Assou shrugs.

Salla stares at his scribbles. "This man you're thinking about," he tells me, wagging his finger at me impatiently. "If you want him, this is the sacrifice you must make: you must buy three guinea fowls. Then you must kill them, cook them, and eat only the wings and necks. In this way, you will have him." He closes his notebook and folds his hands.

"So I can't eat the drumsticks?" I say to Assou.

Assou shrugs. Salla speaks, telling us that the consultation is over. There's nothing about my river trip. Nothing about my getting to Timbuktu.

"I think your guy needs a refresher course," I tell Assou.

"If you would like," Assou offers apologetically, "we can buy guinea fowls in the market."

⌒

I TELL ASSOU THAT I'D LIKE TO SEE THE REAL THING THIS TIME. AN honest-to-God, first-rate sorcerer type. Assou, wanting to win my faith in such people, takes me to see Binta, a Dogon witch living on the outskirts of Mopti in a village called Wailirde. Along the way, we pick up Assou's friend, Barou, who happens to be Peace Corps Baba's younger brother. Barou, a local guide, is also a Dogon by birth and can understand the language. He is quiet and timid, so Assou gladly does the talking for all of us on the way to the village. When we finally arrive in Wailirde, it's after sunset, only a faint orange light coloring the western horizon. Darkness settles on the land, shutting out what light remains and obscuring the shapes of the mud huts. Nothing is lit up in the village, not even a cooking fire. Strangely, the village appears empty, a lone donkey neighing like a banshee into the night.

"Where is everyone?" I ask.

"I don't know," Barou says. "This place scares me."

I follow Assou and Barou into a round adobe hut—Binta's hut. We can barely see where we're going, and we sit down on a wooden bench that faces a dark doorway. A young girl appears out of nowhere, and without saying a word she lights a kerosene lamp, hangs it on a nail nearby, and leaves. It lets out a sickly, scratchy light that barely touches the darkness.

"Where's Binta?" I ask Barou. A Dogon, himself, I'm assuming he knows something about these matters. But he doesn't. He shakes his head and gazes around with apprehension.

Assou nervously smiles and cracks a joke in Bambarra to Barou. They laugh. Their laughing stops all at once, however, as a woman creeps inside the hut.

"Binta," Assou whispers to me.

She appears as just a dark form. I can barely see her at all, except for her hand which reaches out from the darkness. Her voice comes at us, and Barou tells me that she wants payment for her divinatory services. We all drop bills in her hand, and she retreats into the dark room before us. Inside, Barou tells me, are carved ancestor figures— objects so sacred and imbued with magic that no one except Binta and her apprentices are ever allowed to see them.

We hear a gourd rattle being shaken. Binta chants in Dogon in a loud, monotone voice, repeating the same phrase over and over. The effect is hypnotic and powerful. I look to Assou and then to Barou.

"What's she doing now?" I ask them.

Barou tells me he thinks she's contacting the spirit world. Assou is smiling nervously and fingering the sunglasses in his lap.

The sound of the rattle stops. Suddenly, from out of the darkness, comes a screeching voice. It is so angry and high-pitched that Assou and I jump up, terrified. Barou motions for us to calm down. He explains that we're hearing the voice of the *binu*, or spirit. It won't hurt us. It's telling Binta what we need to do in order to dispel evil spirits from our lives and have good fortune. Apparently, a whole slew of evil spirits might bother you at any given time. They build up around a person, so it's important to rid yourself of them periodically, almost like getting an oil change.

It would seem as if we all have quite a number working against us, from the way this binu is screeching at us. I'm struck by how the staccato voice is wholly unlike Binta's, as if a completely different person had materialized in the room. Binta starts asking this binu questions in her own voice, and it responds in a shrieking, impatient way, the words fired out. I keep straining my eyes to see into the dark room before us, to get some glimpse of what's happening inside. I feel as if I'm trapped in some scene from a horror movie, caught as I am in this thick darkness, with frantic, demonic voices screaming at me.

Now a deep male voice booms out—a new binu—its baritone pitch resonating across the hut. This voice, like the other, sounds entirely autonomous from Binta's. It rages and bellows in Bambarra, and Binta interrupts it to ask questions. It fumes back at her with such a loud, ornery list of objections that my ears ring in its wake.

"Which binu is this?" I ask Barou.

He shakes his head. His mouth is open. We three stare at the source of the voices, Binta cajoling them to tell her things, her voice calm yet persistent, while they yell and scold her.

It's interesting how the earlier binu spoke in Dogon, and this one speaks in Bambarra. Binta responds in whichever language they prefer to communicate with, and Barou translates the Dogon words for us. The spirits, he says, are still complaining about the three of us.

Finally, the voices subside. Binta, still in her dark room, tells us what they said: We must all make a "sacrifice." Usually this doesn't have anything to do with killing animals, but rather with "sacrificing" something of value by giving it to someone else. The size of the sacrifice is dependent on the degree of problems that you have and the number of spirits that you've offended. For Barou, he must give away ten kola nuts. Assou must buy some cow's milk and pour it on an active termite mound. Me—well, apparently I've got some work to do. Binta speaks to Barou for a while, and when he finally translates, I feel like I've lost a Monopoly game. I must buy 50 dates and 100 fried rice cakes, and I must give them away to young children or beggars. *Only* to young children or beggars; the children should be under the age of 12.

I ask Barou if Binta will take questions, but he shakes his head. She doesn't field questions to the binu. *They* tell *us* what we need to know, explaining how we can offset angry spirits and evil spells. If I want to get some real answers, I'll have to see a celebrated Muslim *marabout,* a holy man with prophetic powers, whom Barou calls Big Father.

∽

Big Father lives in Manako, east of Mopti. Manako is a typical village of adobe huts sitting in the midst of a dusty savanna of scrub brush and wilted trees. Rain has come later and less often to this region in recent years, the Sahel, or South Sahara, trespassing upon once-fertile farmland, turning it quickly and irrevocably to desert. Prices in Mopti for basic food items have skyrocketed as a result, a single chicken doubling in price, rice prices tripling, the people here wondering how long they can survive the high prices and drought.

Assou is unable to join us today, so I go with Barou in his car. Manako is in the midst of its weekly market when we arrive. Donkey carts crowd the dirt track, loaded with vegetables, fruit, rice. Manako appears fairly prosperous compared to many of the villages we've passed while driving out here, as its huts are intact, and kids don't run around wearing ratty clothes. Still, the pastureland around the village has become a dustbowl.

A man walks by wearing a T-shirt that shows Osama bin Laden's face looking at George W. Bush's; it reads in English: "Politics, not War."

"Is bin Laden popular here?" I ask Barou.

He nods his head. Barou explains that whenever fights break out these days, the most common cause is a disagreement over what happened to New York City on September 11th. Many Malians, Barou says, worship bin Laden like a god and are quick to celebrate the attacks on the United States and to praise the deaths that resulted.

"People are stupid," Barou says, shaking his head. Other Malians to whom I've broached the subject have been much less fervent in their denunciations of bin Laden. When I've asked the question, "What do you think about the September 11 attacks?" the most common response has been, "Look what the Israelis are doing to the Palestinians." Unlike most Malians, Barou considers himself pro-American. This isn't because he's a Dogon animist rather than a Muslim, either. As he and his brother, Peace Corps Baba, run a lucrative business selling African trade beads and Malian tribal art to dealers in the States, the two brothers can attribute much of their wealth to American connections, whereas many Malians have never even met an American in person. It's easy for us to become a concoction of myth or hearsay here, too. Cheap Hollywood flicks show Americans spending all their time machine-gunning bad guys with Arnold Schwarzenegger or cavorting on California beaches in skimpy bathing suits. One of America's greatest contributions to Mali thus far: gangsta rap.

Barou stops his car. We get out and walk past adobe homes to the village's small central square. Before one of the houses, under a shade tree, sits a group of chatting men, all of them facing an old man with a long white beard, dressed in pure white robes: Big Father. He is much lighter-complexioned than most of the men around him, suggesting Arab ancestry. His soft, moist eyes gaze out at me as we approach, and I feel caught in the arresting placidity of his presence. Barou tells me that Big Father is 82 years old—remarkable, as the male life expectancy in Mali is only 51. I sense that there is something truly special about this man.

Marabouts, like Big Father, are all men who possess a strong knowledge of Arabic and the Koran. They are, in effect, Muslim sorcerers: they write magical text for charms; foretell the future; appease wrathful genies; and bring about good fortune through spells. Their work is closely tied to and sanctioned by the Koran, which gives them leave to work with the super-natural realm on behalf of others. For all divinatory requests, the marabout makes use of his Islamic training and customs as a basis for the answers.

In addition to being a marabout, Big Father is also an imam, or prayer leader, at the village mosque; the two métiers often go hand in hand. Barou tells me that some unscrupulous imams become marabouts in order to cash in on the lucrative job of telling people's futures, but the most sincere marabouts are the wealthiest ones because the pro-cess of divination works on a donation basis: the most earnest and suc-cessful individuals receive the largest numbers of devotees, and thus the most money. Big Father is just such a marabout, renowned through-out Mopti for both the integrity and the accuracy of his services.

Big Father ushers us inside his hut, and I sit on a mat opposite him. We look at each other for a moment. I've been wondering if he'd balk at the idea of helping a non-Muslim, but there's nothing but sincerity and generosity in his eyes. He strikes me as a very venerable man. I offer him a generous donation, which he takes humbly, with a nod of the head.

Barou tells me the way it works, that I won't be able to receive answers today. Big Father will take my questions and wait until night, when he will enter into a deep prayer and trance. He will stay up all night, if necessary, until he receives information about my problems. Often, it's in the earliest hours of the morning that he feels his great-est power and a communion with his divinity, at which time he'll be told what I need to do in order to bring about my desires. Barou says that all marabouts work after dark, and that most are descended from previous marabouts. It is a sacred and ancient vocation.

Barou asks Big Father a few of his own questions first. When he fin-ishes, he instructs me to ask my own, translating for me.

I ask: "Will I get to Timbuktu?" I have Barou explain that I'm trav-eling alone by kayak on the Niger and that it's been difficult so far.

Big Father listens patiently to the translation, casting his eyes on me from time to time. When Barou finishes, he nods. He has understood my question, and tonight he will ask it.

He says something and Barou translates: "You have more questions."

"I do?" I say.

Big Father speaks, and Barou translates: "He wants you to tell him what is troubling you."

I hadn't been planning on asking anything else. I guess it's too surreal to me, addressing personal questions to this respectable 82-year-old man sitting before me. I sigh. "I don't know. Just out of curiosity, does he see a man in my near future? You know."

It's a question for some psychic hotline, not a Malian marabout. I feel silly. But I get curious like anyone else.

Big Father nods and waits.

"And then my job," I say, feeling as if I'm on a roll now. "How can I make more money? What can I do? I work hard, so I don't understand what the problem is."

He stares at me with his bright eyes, full of a gentle kindness, as the translation is given.

"That's it," I say.

Big Father nods. He asks for my name, and as I say it he writes it down in Arabic on a piece of paper and checks with me to make sure he's pronouncing it right. He says he will be repeating my name tonight while praying on my behalf. When I return tomorrow, he'll have answers for me.

❦

IT'S THE NEXT MORNING, AND I GO BACK TO SEE BIG FATHER. THIS time I take Assou along, so he can more precisely translate what's said into English. Assou's never seen Big Father and is still partial to Salla, the man who insisted I will have four children some day.

Big Father is in the same place where we found him before, under the shade of a tree, ringed by a small crowd of his devotees. He looks up as we arrive and smiles kindly, getting to his feet. He enters his hut and we follow, taking our shoes off at the door.

Big Father sits on a mat across from us, waiting patiently for the chattering Assou to end a story he's in the middle of telling me. When he finally finishes, Big Father starts speaking, telling Assou the answers he received to my questions. He speaks for a long time, Assou stopping him every once in a while to translate.

"So he says that you'll reach Timbuktu," Assou says. "He's made a saphie for you, to protect you, and he's blessed it."

"This charm will really protect me?" It seems too superstitious a notion to me.

Assou laughs. "Of course," he says.

He listens for a while longer. "Big Father says you have a strange job, and you travel from place to place. He's says you won't make money this way. He says you need to stay in one place and do something there for many months—this is how you'll make money. He's certain of it."

"How does he know about my job?" I ask. Because I never told Barou that I'm a writer, only that I'm traveling in a kayak on the Niger.

Assou asks him, and Big Father nods as he answers.

"He hears these things," Assou says.

I feel a tingling on my neck. For the first time, I'm starting to think that maybe this man has access to some realm most of us don't—*maybe*.

"He heard about them late last night. He asked your questions and prayed for a long time, and a voice told him the answers."

Big Father talks again. Assou starts laughing as he listens.

"This is very interesting, Kira," Assou says. "He's told me about you and men."

"Oh, no. Tell him I don't need to hear about that."

"He said he's seen your life with men. He's seen all the men you've ever been with. He says some of these men were not kind to you, so sometimes you can be … how do you say it?… *paranoid* about men, and you run away. He says you'll get married, but how soon depends on you."

Assou is enjoying this consultation immensely now. As most Malian women get married when they're teenagers, the reason why I'm single has been a source of curiosity and amusement to him ever since we met.

"Big Father says you must be patient with the men you meet, not scared of them. Then you'll meet the right man because you'll let him enter your life, and he will be kind to you. He says you need to stop pushing men away. It all depends on you."

"Great," I say.

It's strange to be told something like this on the plains of West Africa, by an old, white-bearded sorcerer who could have come right out of a Tolkien novel.

Big Father tells me the sacrifice I must make: I need to buy one live sheep and 17 meters of white cloth. Both must be brought to him for a blessing, and then given away to a poor woman. Doing so will help enlist certain divine forces to act on my behalf in all the things I asked him about. He hands me a small, folded piece of paper upon which is written a verse from the Koran: my saphie, meant to protect me during my journey to Timbuktu and beyond. He instructs me to have it sewn inside a leather pouch, which I can wear for good fortune.

I thank him and give him some more money as a gift. How tantalizing it all sounds! White cloth that, when blessed, will correct irregularities in my life. A live sheep that will bring love and prosperity and safety. A saphie to ward off evil with magic words. Fifty dates given away here, a hundred rice cakes there, to send away malign spirits. If only life were so efficiently regulated. If only so easily understood. I hold the saphie in my palm and stare at the folded paper. How badly I want to believe it holds some power, some efficacy beyond what I can comprehend.

I thank Big Father and get up, promising to send him some white cloth and a sheep for his blessing—as long as he assures me that the sheep won't be killed. He reassures me that all will be well for me—though, as he's said, much will depend on me. He will be praying for me. He hopes I will like Timbuktu.

CHAPTER EIGHT

~⁀

ASSOU TELLS ME THAT HE'S JUST BEEN TOLD THE LOCATION OF ONE of the most powerful witches in all of Mali, in case I'm interested. Her name is Yatanu, and she lives in the midst of Dogon country, in a tiny village called Niry in the Bandiagara Escarpment, a few hours southeast of Mopti. I feel a bit witched-out at the moment, but he assures me that I've never seen the likes of this woman. When she was ten, her parents, witches themselves, cut open her left arm and put a scarab beetle into the biceps, sewing the skin back up. Presumably the beetle died, but a spirit named *deguru* remained, with whom she converses to obtain knowledge about people's pasts and futures. She can also summon up the power of her beetle spirit in order to bring about particular events, so that most Dogon people live in terror of her.

I admit it sounds impressive. I tell Assou that I'll hire a Land Rover to take us out there. I'm fascinated by the idea of someone having a monopoly of power over other people's lives.

The Dogon living around the escarpment are mostly animists,

having protected their beliefs from invading Islamic armies by retreating into the rugged, rocky country of eastern Mali. Here they constructed adobe huts high in the cliff walls, not unlike modern-day Anasazi, allowing them to continue their traditions virtually unmolested. To this day, they remain proud and suspicious of outsiders, rumors abounding that they still conduct human sacrifices—a fairly commonplace practice for them not so very long ago. Park himself wrote about a people living in this part of Mali, known for their cannibalism, and it's quite possible he was talking about the Dogon: "To the best information I was able to collect," Park wrote, "[the inhabitants] are cruel and ferocious; carrying their resentment toward their enemies, so far as never to give quarter; and even to indulge themselves with unnatural and disgusting banquets of human flesh."

Rain has come to the Dogon country of Mali more often than around Mopti, and the usually dry, inhospitable terrain has turned to a verdant landscape. Groves of squat, bulbous baobab trees open enormous red flowers to the sun. The distant mountains of the Bandiagara Escarpment shimmer with fresh green shoots. Here is the view often associated with the sub-Saharan plains of Africa: acacias, savanna, monkeys scampering into brush. The Sahara hasn't taken over this greenery yet, though I know that the desert country lies disturbingly close to the north.

As we travel the dirt track to the escarpment, I have the driver of the Land Rover stop at every poor village or congregation of kids I see along the road so I can pass out some of my 100 rice cakes and 50 dates. Per Binta the witch's instructions, I make sure I only give them to beggars, or kids under 12. It took Assou and me a couple of hours this morning simply to procure enough of the cakes from street vendors, so that I was seriously thinking of just forgetting this whole "sacrifice" business, but Assou insisted I not offend the spirits by ignoring their orders. Meanwhile, I had Barou drop off the 17 meters of white cloth and the sheep with Big Father. It's been a long and expensive day of appeasing spirits and obtaining blessings. I much prefer my Buddhism.

I've discovered, though, that I'm really enjoying fulfilling my sacrifice duties. I give out goodies to little girls balancing huge bundles of washing on their heads, and to young boys gathering firewood in the dusty savanna. This is poor country, and the dates and rice cakes are Mopti city luxuries that they probably never have out here. We pass a field where some skinny, malnourished-looking kids are herding goats. I order the car stopped so I can fill their arms with rice cakes. Our driver, an enormous, bullish man who would make a great linebacker, steps out of the car to call to the kids. They run off in terror, hiding behind rocks. I send Assou instead, and pretty soon the kids are surrounding the car, smiling and thanking me with outspread hands. It takes a while before I'm able to give everything away, and I see that behind the obvious superstition of this practice, behind my skepticism and left-brain resistance, is the act itself: basic generosity between people. Nothing silly or irrational about it.

We decide to spend the night in a large Dogon village called Banini, which rests on the edge of the escarpment. Assou and I make arrangements to visit the Dogon witch first thing tomorrow. This village is well-frequented by packs of tourists during the cool months of the winter season, as it sits beside an impressively high waterfall that plummets hundreds of feet to grassy slopes below. Though Banini sees few people this time of year, its collection of tourist shops remains open for business, full of the kind of low-quality kitsch that foreigners must buy in large enough quantities to persuade the local people to keep making the stuff: crude masks of fertility figures, Bambarra antelope carvings, wooden key chains. I can't escape the incessant solicitations from the store owners and so enter each place for a brief look. The most widely sold items are imitations of Dogon granary doors. Obtaining a genuine antique door has long been a coup for African art collectors, so that the best way to find one is not to go to the Dogon villages anymore but to art galleries or private homes in the West. The doors are renowned for their representation of ancestral figures, but the imitation ones improve upon the features and are more elaborately carved. The theory seems to be: give the tourist more bang for his buck. I see a pile of newly carved doors lying in the grass behind a Dogon hut. They're left out in the sun and rain for a few months until the wood warps and gets stained by mildew, giving off the appearance of something ancient and sacred.

I walk with Assou through Banini village, staring at ancient Tellem ruins in the crevices of cliffs higher up. The Tellem were the former occupiers of this land until the Dogon came along, driving them into extinction. It's not known what happened exactly, the Tellem vanishing but for their decaying cliff dwellings littering the countryside. The Dogon now use these homes as places to deposit their dead. Tourists frequently sign up for Tellem tours, the highlight of which is visiting some of the more accessible mud dwellings to see the human bones within.

What's left of the Tellem people's culture—some old bronze sculptures, fetish figures, burial necklaces made of crude iron links attached to centuries-old trade beads of glass and stone—are sold to tourists in a hush-hush sort of way by local Dogon entrepreneurs. Most of these things were obtained by grave-robbing, which involves rappelling down cliff faces with crude baobab bark ropes and raiding the crumbling adobe structures, but the Dogon express little repentance in face of the great financial incentives. This way of making spare change has become commonplace enough to require more daring maneuvers into higher, harder to reach crevices, as well as scouting the surrounding countryside for new caches of artifacts. If one village runs out, another farther down the escarpment has probably found something.

Banini is a typical Dogon village in that it's built among the rocks of the escarpment, each squat adobe hut having its own little courtyard and a cylindrical granary building topped with a cone of thatch. *Cute* is the word that comes to mind. The village looks cute and benign, like a kind of hobbit land, with its granaries of different sizes—tall ones for men's food, short ones for women's—built among huge boulders. It sits at the base of that high waterfall that plummets down the rock face and pools beside a few baobab trees in full bloom. I'm hesitant to use the word "Eden" to describe this place, but it does look very pristine and untouched, very innocent. Goats wander the hard-packed earth, being chased by naked children. The kids' umbilical cords were cut a couple of inches from their bellies so that their navels literally sprout an additional appendage. An old chief sits in an open-air meetinghouse, called a *toguna*, that's covered with a low millet-stalk roof. The roof is designed in such a way so as to prevent anyone from getting enflamed during a village squabble and standing up to make angry threats. Every year the toguna gets a new roof of millet stalks on top of the previous layer, so that it resembles a Chinese pagoda.

I follow Assou around the village, and he talks and talks endlessly. He does it with the intention of being helpful, as he knows a lot about Dogon country, but by keeping my attention on what he's saying, I constantly miss the scenery. I haven't gotten the chance to just be present. I sit down on a log and stop listening to him finally, taking in the beauty of this place—its waterfall, the enormous red flowers that fall from the branches of the baobabs like autumnal leaves.

The Dogon believe that everyone is born twice. The first birth is our entry into mortal life, replete with its struggles and hardship. But during this experience, we can have a moment of "sight," becoming aware of a state known as the *sigi*, or second birth. When you experience this sigi birth, you will never be the same. You have seen another world, one beyond time. You know the feeling of transcendental knowledge, the cause for all things, and there is no going back. The Dogon believe that the sigi birth must happen to all of us, if we are to become whole. There is no time to spare. No time for dallying. The path awaits.

Understandably, the Dogon believe that the "road of the sigi" is a long, arduous undertaking, and so every 60 years the Dogon villages in these parts commence a special five-year-long ceremonial period designed to help people "see the sigi" through dance and ritual. Such is the importance of knowing a wisdom greater than oneself. There seem to be equivalents of the sigi in Western and Eastern religions. In Christianity, particularly its mystical tradition, it might be seen as progressing through the "beautiful mansions" to ultimate union with God, as described by St. Teresa of Avila. In Judaism, it is like the pursuit of the Kabbalist, following the 12 stages of the *tzaddik* (righteous person) to the "throne of God" and a realization of truth. In Buddhism and Hinduism, it is akin to the transformational understanding of non-duality, selflessness, and the impermanence of all things. But regardless of how a religion might explain its own experience of "rebirth," the goal seems to be the same: transcendence of self and a joining with universal truth.

∽

I RETURN WITH ASSOU TO THE GUESTHOUSE WHERE WE'RE STAYING, telling him I'm going to take a walk for a while—alone. Silence is like music to me, and I need some time to myself. Like me, Mungo Park was usually quite reticent, though every person of any importance in London wanted to have the famous explorer at his or her dinner table after Park's narrative became a bestseller. Still, it was reported that the great discoverer of the Niger River detested small talk and had no interest in attending dinner parties or being publicly acknowledged for his achievements, leading a spurned London hostess to say that Park had "the manner and dignities of his Niger kings." Good for Park.

I walk up a rocky hill and sit to watch the sun set behind the escarpment. I breathe in the stillness, feeling a peace settling upon me that's otherwise hard to find in Mali. Even when I paddle on the river, there's always somebody around—a Somono fisherman in a distant canoe, village people on shore, a sheep herder staring at me from the edge of the riverbank. It's a luxury just to be alone for a while, having nothing to listen to except the sounds that come at me from the evening's quiet. I think of the Dogon idea of second birth; I imagine never being able to see the world around me in the same way again.

I return to the guesthouse. Assou finds me, asking if I'm angry with him.

I insist that I'm not. "People aren't all the same," I explain. "I just need to be alone sometimes." But I get tired of trying to explain to some people that I value privacy and solitude as much as they value socializing. If I don't have time to myself each day, I get stir-crazy. I'll just run off, needing to escape from a place. But in countries like Mali, with strong tribal traditions, that must sound virtually incomprehensible, as family, religion, and social order provide a crucial structure that sustains people and prevents discontent. Back home, being alone might be considered a kind of independence, but here it is pathology.

We reach Niry village, where the witch Yatanu lives. It sits high on a rocky plateau, a collection of low adobe dwellings mingling with tall, thatch-topped granaries. Dogon women crouch in the tiny, beehive-like menstruation huts to protect the village from the devilry of their periods. I imagine being one of them, stuck in the hot huts once a month, banished and accursed for being female. Assou instructs me to carefully follow the path that he takes, as walking arbitrarily might cause me to step on some taboo spot of ground and call forth the wrath of spirits. Little Dogon boys gape at us: this isn't a village that ever sees tourists.

We climb up the rocky slope to the huts perched above, searching for Yatanu's. Assou has never met this woman, but he says he's heard about her: she's at least 70 years old, is one of the Dogon's most powerful and feared witches. It's hard to get a consultation with her because she doesn't like most of her visitors and sends them away, but I've brought along a village officer who happens to be related to her, hoping he'll help the cause.

We stop at a mud hut, and the Dogon man walks inside. After a short moment, Yatanu appears before us: a toothless and wizened woman, breasts lying flat against her chest, scrappy indigo sarong tied about her bony waist. She stands in the shadows of her hut, staring at me. Assou tells her that I'm here to ask for a consultation, and will she grant me one?

She steps forward into the sunlight, sits down on her haunches, and studies me. I smile at her nervously, looking into her cataracted eyes. She says something in Dogon to the man I've brought along, who then translates to Assou, who translates to me: "She likes you."

Sighs all around. I give her a wad of money in gratitude, which makes her face erupt into a grin.

"She likes you even more," Assou whispers.

I ask my question: "Will I be able to get to Timbuktu?"

She puckers her lips and nods as the question is translated. She places her left arm tightly against her chest and speaks to the muscle where the beetle spirit supposedly lives. All at once, something on the biceps leaps up and hops around. I've never seen such a thing, nor has Assou—our mouths are hanging open. I lean forward to look for scars on her arm, but see nothing.

"That's too weird," I say to Assou, an object now seeming to strain and lurch beneath the skin, as if trying to escape. It's about the shape of a large-sized gumball, and the movements are so severe that I find myself taking a step back.

Yatanu reports her findings to me: "You'll get to Timbuktu."

Assou asks some questions of his own now, and whenever the answer is yes, the muscle leaps up and dances.

"I'll ask her if you'll ever get married," Assou says to me, grinning.

"Don't ask her that," I say.

"It's too late! She says you will. This man will be from your country. She says she is asking Ama for special help with this."

I ask who Ama is, and it turns out that he is the head Dogon deity, who speaks through the beetle spirit intermediary in her arm. As most Dogon are animists, it's not surprising that they have an entire pantheon at their disposal, but Ama is the head honcho, a deity of fickle temperament who demands constant propitiation. Below him are other gods, like Lewe, god of the earth, who reveals himself as a snake, as well as Nomo, god of the water. Then there are a whole slew of lesser spirits: *yeneu* enter people and exchange body parts; evil *atywunu* live in the brush around a village and have been known to attack people. *Yeba* spirits live just outside a village as well, but are less dangerous, while the *jinu* roam throughout the countryside, ambushing unsuspecting travelers. All these spirits, in addition to the gods themselves, require such care and respect that it couldn't be an easy thing keeping yourself secure and everybody happy in the spirit world. Just to be on the safe side, many Dogon men carry around a magical horsehair switch, which they use to fend off spirits.

Yatanu says that she wants me to know a few things. The first is that she's Ama's elite messenger among mortals. She has a close relationship with him and has personally asked him for things on my behalf: success reaching Timbuktu, help with bringing the right man to me for marriage, and general prosperity. She says that with the assistance of Ama and his helpers there is no doubt of these things happening. When one thing comes true, I must send thanks to her, which she will then send on to the gods on my behalf. It is customary that I show my gratitude for the gods' intercession by also sending her a gift—be it money or women's clothes or whatever. But the point is this: when the gods help you in life, you must show them your appreciation; if you don't, you will offend them and they might spoil whatever has manifested in your life.

She also wants me to know that she's doing me a favor by allowing me to see her. Such consultations cost a Dogon witch days, weeks, even months of her life. Each time she performs a divination, she loses some of her life span by way of payment to the spirits. Also, she's not only shown the future of her clients each time, but also her *own* future, including her death. Thus, it can be frightening to perform any divinations at all, but Yatanu knows that this is her duty in life, and so she obeys the path she's been given. She declares that she's not scared of her calling.

Yatanu answers some of Assou's own questions, and he starts looking very pleased. "She says I will make a lot of money," he tells me with a flash of a grin, turning back to her.

I'm wondering how reliable beetle spirits are. But not wanting to further deplete Yatanu's life span by more questions, I ask Assou if we can leave.

He agrees. He's looking a bit troubled now. "I think," he says, "it's not good for us to speak to any more witches. We've spoken to enough."

"You'd be right about that," I say.

We watch the beetle spirit hopping around in Yatanu's arm.

"A lot of witches have helped us with their power," Assou says. "Many spirits have been called upon, you know? This is dangerous power. I think we shouldn't see any more people. And you must remember to give each witch a gift in the future, to show your appreciation when things start to happen. This is very important."

"Okay," I say.

Yatanu goes inside her hut for a moment. She comes out with a small wooden carving and hands it to me. It looks not unlike one of the faces carved on Easter Island.

She speaks, and Assou gets the translation from the Dogon man. "This is a good luck charm for you," Assou says. "It will protect you whenever you carry it with you. It will help you on all your travels." And now Assou laughs. "Yatanu likes you very much. What did you do to her?"

CHAPTER NINE

⌣

IT'S TIME FOR THE JOURNEY TO CONTINUE: TIMBUKTU OR BUST. I estimate I'm about two weeks away, give or take a day. That's roughly 350 miles left to paddle. *Jesus*, I think. *Three hundred fifty miles.* My respite in Mopti has spoiled me, and I find myself resisting all the uncertainties that lie ahead, clinging to the comfort and security found in town. By now I feel qualified to make some predictions about what will come: much hotter temperatures, hippos galore, and the difficult crossing of Lake Debo. And then, of course, there will always be the mercurial moods of the Niger. Something Mungo Park wrote echoes my thoughts: "All these circumstances crowded at once on my recollection; and I confess that my spirits began to fail me." Or try to fail me, if I let them.

Rémi meets me in the hotel lobby early in the morning, eager to take advantage of the good lighting for his photographs. He looks well fed and in a chipper mood. For him, today is the continuation of what has amounted to a river safari on the Niger. He insists on putting my inflated kayak in his boat, so he can shuttle me back to

the town dock where there are more picturesque crowds and mar-
ketplace hustle-bustle for the background of his shots. All I want to
do is *really* leave, get this trip under way again. I'm like a runner sitting in before-game limbo, nerves getting frayed. But I humor him,
getting in his boat and backtracking a mile to the docks where I put
my kayak in the water. I paddle back and forth past the crowds gathering on shore. I try to look like Serious Kayaker, like Hardened
Adventurer Leaving Mopti. Whatever such a person would look like.
I career past the pirogues tied to the piers, waving at the kids, waving at the fruit vendors and fishermen and salt sellers, feeling like
some goddamn goodwill ambassador. I feel really stupid.

Rémi's pinasse circles behind me as he takes pictures with several different cameras. He calls out directions—paddle that way, paddle toward him, paddle by the crowd over there. I do it all, over and
over, and at last he gets enough Mopti shots for the magazine's needs
and bids me a prompt goodbye, best wishes on the Niger, and I'm
not sure when or where I'll run into him again.

My five-day break in Mopti reveals itself in slower paddle strokes,
my stamina not up to peak strength as when I first arrived in town,
but I know this will soon change. The weather has been holding up
so far, and I don't have to battle any fierce winds. But in its place
are the fishermen's nets, which I hadn't counted on. Back by Old
Ségou, the river was so wide that this hadn't been a problem, but
by Mopti the Niger is about a third the width, so men string their
nets across nearly the whole river. They only move them for the rare
river barge, meaning that I have to pass over each one I come
across. Often, I can't see any net below the water and don't realize
I've hit one until my kayak's rudder gets caught, yanking me back.
The nets like to get caught in the rudder's screws, meaning I have
to jump into the river and tread water, trying to untangle the mess.

This is tedious, but my real worry is that the fishermen who own the net are going to see and get pissed off. Or—God forbid—some hippos will find me instead. I still haven't shaken my fear of them, perhaps because the fear is actually a reasonable one out here. I get things untangled as quickly as possible and jump into my boat, as if this craft of rubber and air can protect me from two-ton beasts.

I spend the morning paddling and untangling myself from nets, my progress pathetically slow. I can still see Mopti's radio tower behind me, faintly visible. When I take off the rudder, my boat flies all over the place and I can barely steer. As even the slightest breeze sends me swirling, I put it back on again. Without that rudder, I realize, I would have never been able to do this trip; Timbuktu would have remained just another mysterious name on a map.

I go more slowly, staying on the lookout for nets, pushing them down with my paddle and crossing over them, or paddling around the larger ones, even if this means crossing the entire river. This amuses the fishermen, who are usually sitting in a canoe somewhere close to shore, watching; but as soon as a big river barge starts speeding up the river, they race to pull in their nets. In this way, I pass village after village, some largely populated with adobe homes, some with a mere hut or two. The people come out to stare at me. Sometimes they're friendly and open, waving as I pass; other times they merely stand there and watch me go by, demanding I come over and give them money, or *cadeaux*. This latter reaction is relatively new. During the first part of my trip, all people really wanted was to ask me questions or yell out greetings. But north of Mopti, barges frequently tote tourists to Timbuktu, two to three days distant by motorized boat. And so I become yet another of the wealthy tourists going by.

◡

IT'S NEARLY THREE O'CLOCK, AND THE WESTERN SKY IS STARTING TO turn dark red. Blood red. Black clouds block out the sun, giving a taste of dusk to the early afternoon. A violent wind begins churning the waters of the Niger, sending large waves and spray against me. Panicked birds shoot across the river, screeching. Herds of goats buck and stampede on shore, and all fishing canoes leave the water. It's as if Armageddon is coming. I can tell already that this storm is going to be much worse than anything I've seen yet on the Niger. Which is saying a lot. I have to get off this river—fast.

Mungo Park called these storms, "tornadoes," which was hardly an exaggeration. His second trip took place in the midst of the rainy season, and he blamed the weather for the death of so many of his soldiers. His letters from that journey are littered with accounts of being stuck in violent deluges. At one point, he wrote:

> We were overtaken by a very heavy tornado, which wet us completely.... The ground all round was covered with water about three inches deep.... The tornado had an instant effect on the health of the soldiers, and proved to us to be the *beginning of sorrow*. I had proudly flattered myself that we should reach the Niger with a very moderate loss.... But now the rain had set in, and I trembled to think that we were only half way through our journey. The rain had not commenced three minutes before many of the soldiers were affected with vomiting, while others fell asleep as if half intoxicated.

I keep thinking about that line of Park's—"proved to us to be the *beginning of sorrow*." He even underscored the words. I can feel his dread, can see it now in the clouds taking over the sky. I struggle to get to shore, careful not to be caught off-guard and flipped over by one of the large waves.

The dark clouds spread across the sky, extinguishing the last patches of light. I pull in to the nearest village. There's no time to be circumspect about where I stop; I can only hope these people will be welcoming. The village is sizable and has its own mud mosque. As there are no Fulani cattle around, the people are most likely Bozos. I think of the last Bozo village I was at, Koa, and the Osama bin Laden poster hanging up in the middle of town, and the crowds that had to be beaten back with sticks. I've come to fear Bozo villages.

As I paddle my kayak onto shore, kids surround me, adults running to see who I am. Before long, I'm aware of something being off about this village, something not feeling right.

I ask them where I am, and the people yell, "Wameena!"

"Where's your chief?"

They point to a nearby tree.

"Where are you going in this boat?" one man asks loudly in French.

"Timbuktu," I tell him.

He yells this to the crowd in Bambarra, and a great uproar ensues.

"Timbuktu?" the man asks. "Are you crazy?"

"Probably," I say.

And now I think I understand what's strange about this place. Everyone shouts here. It's a shouting village. No one speaks at a normal volume. I ask what people they are, and they tell me Bozo. I sigh. Pulling my kayak onshore, I hoist my backpack onto a shoulder and squeeze my way through the crowd, asking for an audience with the chief.

The sky becomes a deeper, darker maroon as the wind picks up. I follow the French-speaking man to the village. Several kids pick up my kayak and carry it behind me, as if it were an additional piece of my baggage. Along the way, the crowd is so close that I'm being constantly bumped and jostled: I've become the town freak show. The kids keep up a chant in the only French they've seemed to learn: "*Donnez-moi l'argent! Donnez-moi l'argent!*" Give me money! Give me money! Which tells me that this place has seen its share of tourists, probably from Mopti. One enterprising kid, a boy whose parents sent him to an Islamic boarding school in Nigeria, asks me for money in English. He also informs me that he's making himself my translator. Whether I need one or not.

I meet the chief in a small courtyard behind the village's mud mosque. He appears to be a friendly man, a trait augmented by the money I hand him as a gift. He breaks into a smile and immediately deposits my backpack and kayak in one of the rooms of his large adobe house. He urges the crowd to leave me alone—which they do, for the most part, people backing away. No one leaves the courtyard, though, which by now doesn't surprise me.

One of the chief's wives comes over and asks me, shouting, if I'd like dinner tonight and if rice would suffice. I still can't get over how everyone shouts here. I've been to my share of villages around the world—ones deep in the jungles of Borneo and New Guinea, ones hidden in the rice paddies of Bangladesh—and this is first time I've experienced such a phenomenon. I thank her, giving her some money. Outside the courtyard, the coming storm has started ripping and tearing across the countryside, threshing the manes of donkeys and sending clouds of dust into our faces. The red clouds slowly engulf the village, and people lose their curiosity about me, staring up fearfully at the sky.

The rain comes all at once, hard, like a punishment. The drops flail our skin, and everyone runs into the nearest hut—everyone but me. I want to see this storm. I leave the courtyard for an open field beside the village. For once, no crowd is around me and no one approaches.

The storm has granted me a reprieve from the stares, at the price of a wind that nearly knocks me over. I guard my eyes from the moving vortexes of dust, which swirl and twist through the passageways of the village like genies come to life.

The Niger flows backward, large whitecaps assailing the shore, causing the tied-up canoes to strike each other with loud, hollow thumps. I've never seen a storm as bad as this one—not even back home, growing up in the Midwest. The rain stings my skin, soaking my already river-dampened clothes. Thunder doesn't offer the occasional boom, but consumes the entire sky with noise, so that the earth quakes and vibrates with apocalyptic vengeance.

"Hoo-eee!" I yell into the might of it all. There's something about the power of this storm, the magnificence of it, that fills me. Nothing bothers me anymore. Nothing scares me. It's just me and the world, meeting head-on. "Hey, Mun-go!" I yell. "Mun-go Park!"

The village people stare out of their huts at me. I let the violent winds hold me up and twirl me around. They try to tear my skirt and shirt from me, try to knock me down. The people point across the river to a particularly bad wind that's tearing up soil and spraying it into the Niger. The violent wind hits trees nearby, trying to pull off branches. It whips my hair about my face and knocks me to my knees. I wait. I don't feel any fear, only curiosity. I wonder what's going to happen next.

After several minutes, the storm loses strength and releases me from the grip of its winds. I feel as if I've been returned to earth. I walk back to one of the huts, passing a man squatting silently in a corner of the courtyard, his clothes soaked from the rain. The boy who has commissioned himself as my translator comes forward to explain that this man is "stupid and crazy"—the village outcast. I look at him again: He sits as if in his own world, his expression peaceful though the world around him just threatened to blow him away. As the storm renews its strength, the chief runs out to pull the crazy man into shelter, putting him beside me. I glance at him, envious of his unperturbed face. We all wait and watch. For calamity? For death? No one is speaking. Even for the people of Wameena, who have lived here all their lives, this is a bad storm.

At last, the storm discharges its fury to the east of us, taking the bloody skies with it. The adobe homes have lost a great part of their walls, clay trickling away in the streams of water that escape from the courtyards. The women immediately get to work, bringing out large pails of dry river clay and patching the parts of their homes that have fallen in. The chief smiles benignly at me and shrugs. Just another storm. The children start begging for money from me again, the surest sign that normality has returned.

While the chief's wives cook dinner for his large extended family, I sit in a chair in the courtyard and look around. I feel changes taking place in me, yet it's hard for me to pinpoint how or what. My thoughts are a jumble in my head, and I still feel electrified by the strength of the storm. I think of how I struggled for hours today to untangle my boat from the fishnets. I keep wanting everything to go *my* way on this trip, without delays or mishaps or defeats. But when I stood in the storm just now, an extraordinary thing occurred: all fear left me, and with it, all demands for the way things should be. I stood there as the earth fired out everything, the worst it had. And to my great surprise, the show ended. It passed.

There are times when I'm traveling when I forget that things pass, and then the so-called benefits of an experience elude me, and I can think only of the difficulties. I find it hard to appreciate anything with the sweat running off my face and burning my eyes, the sun's heat scorching my skin, my body aching from holding the paddle. What room for "experience" when there is only a wish to get to the next place faster, so that the end might be nearer?

I stare at the Mali I see around me—the chickens pecking at wet clay, naked children walking through mud puddles. The goats on the riverbanks look at me accusingly, as if I had somehow caused the storm. A crowd gathers nearby to stare at me, the kids asking me for money in incessant whispers. There are just too many of them to give money to. And beyond that, what would I be teaching them? Only the same lessons the other tourists have: that white people represent money and nothing more. Maybe it's foolish, wishful thinking that I want to be more to the people I meet. It seems crucial that I become more, that we understand each other, know the commonality of our existence, know how we can help one another. But here in Wameena we have only a single night together, and the women are busy patching houses and cooking, and the men are discussing plans, language difficulties separating us more easily than continents ever can, and with much more finality. So here, too, is something I should probably learn to accept.

I offer to help the women repair their houses, but they laugh and wave me away, so I sit down to write. Sometimes when I travel I'll remember what I left behind in the States, those things I used to think about all the time, as if they deserved the full weight attributed to them by my mind. (The children are surrounding me, watching the cryptic scribbles coming from my pen. The boy with the English is demanding I go to the local market and buy him a camera. *A camera*, he insists.) I think of all sorts of things. The journey does this. The moment I take a rest, it steps in to remind me of where I've been, not just where I'm going. Inevitably, I think of the past relationships of my life, wondering what happens to the feelings that people have for each other. And why does lost love feel like a kind of death? But what place for such thoughts *here*, *now*, in Wameena village, among the chattering kids demanding money, and the yelling adults? Those times feel as evanescent as the storm that came and passed on the Niger this afternoon. In a moment my mind forgets them for other things. Like the sight of the village women repairing their adobe houses. Like the crazy man, who once more crouches outside, looking for the storm that left him behind. I see the clay caked to my sandals, the damp shirt I wear, the rooster that has mistaken dusk for dawn and crows into the coming night.

⤳

I EAT DINNER WITH THE CHIEF'S WIVES, ALTERNATING BETWEEN slapping mosquitoes and bringing handfuls of rice to my mouth. People in Mali traditionally eat with their fingers, so they always rinse their hands in a bowl of water before they start. The right hand is used for putting food in the mouth; the left, meant for sanitary cleaning only, is kept at one's side. There is no use of toilet paper whatsoever, so the indispensable left hand and a jug of water must fulfill all hygienic purposes. Being a lefty, I frequently forget which hand is for what when I eat, shocking hosts and causing a ruckus at nearly every village I've been to.

I listen to the women chatting—or I should say shouting—to each other in Bambarra. While we eat, a TV man arrives from upriver. He brings with him a large color TV, an antenna, and a portable gas generator, setting these things up on a table in the middle of the chief's courtyard. It is technology and modernity come to Wameena for a rare evening's entertainment, and the entire town packs in to watch the show. I sit in the midst of the throng, my expectations as high as everyone else's, the excitement among us palpable.

It is a long wait, as the equipment must be set up and made to run, and it's an old, unruly TV. At last the set is turned on. We lean forward to try to discern shapes from the fuzzy images, while the TV man makes a final, impressive adjustment that brings color and sound all at once, leaping out of the set into the starlit village.

No movies come on. No Bruce Lee or Rambo taking on the world. Here in Wameena, we watch nothing but Malian commercials and public health service announcements. There are advertisements for luxury hotels in Bamako, showing large swimming pools with turquoise waters, smiling attendants, contented white customers in suits and ties. Cameras pan over banquet feasts, where Malian businessmen toast each other and gleeful families skip across posh halls.

The little naked children around me watch this, mouths ajar, eyes transfixed on images that must be utterly foreign and fantastical to them. They see shots of white women with blond hair, not unlike mine, wearing pretty dresses, high heels, gold jewelry. They see impressive luxury cars pulling up before the chandeliered hallways, emitting Malian families on holiday.

At last the commercials give way—not to a movie, though, but to a Malian woman demonstrating how to wash one's hands. She speaks in French, urging viewers to prevent the spread of infectious disease, holding up a bar of soap before vigorously washing her hands under a village pump. The people around me watch this with the same rapt attention they gave to the commercials. Movies, if there are any, don't come, but I see that just having the TV is the point. Having the images to watch, the scenes to marvel over. Unlike me, everyone appears absolutely content with whatever comes.

⌒

I SEE RÉMI'S BOAT PARKED ALONG A BARREN SHORE, NEAR THE RUIN of an adobe house. He stands and waves to me, and I paddle over to him. He and Heather rest on cushioned benches under the shade of the boat's canopy, their cook preparing dinner for everyone. He tells me they've had fish for the past two meals, and so they stopped at every village along the river, trying to buy some chickens. But to no avail—no one has chickens to sell.

I try to commiserate. I offer him a shake of the head.

"This is a French boat," Rémi says. "You see? The cuisine is very important."

I laugh. "I've noticed."

I feel culture shock every time I come across Rémi's boat. Just his talk about the day's menu. And then everyone inside looks so *clean*. They wear dry clothes, drink from bottles of mineral water. I glance at my own sweaty clothes, my mud-smeared bottles of filtered water tasting of iodine tablets.

As if reading my mind, Rémi offers me a bottle of water and invites me inside to rest. I try to find a way to climb in without getting their things wet or sullying their boat cushions. My sandals are hopelessly covered with river clay; my clothes are soaked with the river water that I splash on myself to try to cool off; and with all my sweating I don't smell like daisies these days. It's strange to suddenly care about cleanliness and propriety, as being muddy and sweaty and wet have become such a part of this trip that anything otherwise would feel abnormal.

I take my sandals off and lie down on a bench in his boat, closing my eyes. It's the first time all day that I've had the sun off me, and for a moment I forget what world I'm in. With the mineral water, sizzling fish, and French fries (with ketchup, no less, or mayonnaise if I prefer) awaiting everyone for dinner, I can't be entirely sure *where* I am. All I do know is that if I can manage to stick around long enough for dinner, there's a good chance they'll feed me.

Rémi asks me if I'd like a Coke or a Fanta. He has Orange Fanta or Apple Fanta. But there is also beer.

"You have Fanta?" I can't believe it.

He points to a large clay pot, which is filled with cold water to keep the bottles inside cool. "Orange or apple?"

"Uh, orange," I say. The order is sent back to the cook, and sure enough, a cold bottle of honest-to-God Orange Fanta appears from the giant clay pot and is handed to me.

It turns out that this boat is fully stocked with Coke, Fanta, beer, and bottled water, so that finding Rémi feels like coming upon a kind of minibar in the middle of the South Sahara.

Rémi explains his plan to me. He'd like to take some "bivouac" shots of me—Kira by Her Tent, Kira Writing in Her Journal by the River, et cetera. And, hopefully, if the weather turns bad, he can also get Kira Plaintively Surveying the River. He's chosen this spot because he likes the adobe ruin nearby. He was thinking, if I wouldn't mind, of having me set up my tent next to it.

I study the ruin. It's very poetic, in a grim sort of way. "Bleak," I say. And it occurs to me that such an adjective wouldn't be far off when it comes to describing parts of my trip. Bleak. Yes. Kira Enjoying a Bleak Trip.

Rémi smiles. I shrug. What the hell. I know that there are certain types of shots he must get of me, a kind of checklist. Gear shots. Tent shots. Paddling shots. Native-interaction shots. And now, bleak shots.

We wait until the sun is starting to set and the good lighting arrives, and I go on shore to set up my "bivouac." I put up my tent smack next to the ruin and hang my wet clothes on its sides to dry. At Rémi's request, I carry my kayak from where it's docked in the river and put it alongside my tent, laying it out in such a way that it looks photogenic to him. He asks me to take out my map of Mali, so now I become Kira Intently Studying Her Map. A local girl finds us, and Rémi gives her some candy and sweet-talks her into holding my kayak paddle. He's got a way with the kids out here, could rival Mr. Rogers, and pretty soon he's got the terror-stricken girl holding my paddle and smiling feebly at the strange tubab with all the cameras. I sit near her in various poses, per Rémi's instructions, and try to look Adventurous.

At last, he announces that he "has the shots" and declares an end to the photo shoot. He pretends to find a hidden piece of candy in his shirt pocket and produces it for the girl as a parting present. I quickly make my escape, to write. Writing in my journal is the one thing I always enjoy on my trips, the one thing I count on for rest and comfort. I wander down to the shore, the mud bank rising some ten feet from the water so that I have a special vantage point from which to watch the sun set over the river. I find a little nook in the bank, out of sight of the others in the boat and the fields behind me, and insert myself inside. I sigh and shut my eyes. Even at six o'clock, the sun is hot and scalding. I pull my hat low on my head and lean back. My journal rests in my lap, but I don't write yet. I just want to breathe in the peace for a while.

I think about today. What of it? Just a lot of paddling. Virtually nonstop. Nine hours' worth of paddling. And the heat, as usual. And the aching of my arms and hands. And the feeling of foolishness that I ever decided to do such a trip, and also the gratitude for all I've seen and learned. But mostly the exhaustion. Rémi told me he's photographed other people who have taken similarly "physically challenging" trips, and he's wondered if such people lose sight of the beauty around them. It had struck me as a retaliation of sorts, as if I had just pointed out to him the relaxing way he's decided to do his own trip on the Niger. I admitted that yes, at times I forget to see the beauty for all my sweating and paddling and exhaustion. What I did not say was that beauty doesn't forget me, that it intrudes even in the midst of my slow, often tedious way of travel. It surprises me in clouds of birds shooting across an early morning sky outside Mopti. Or shows up in the white butterflies struggling across the Niger, beating fragile wings. Or in all these evenings spent in thatch-hut villages, the nights dazing me with stars. It is beauty enough for me. Too much beauty, at times, so that I must shut my eyes to it all.

I hear a familiar clicking sound: Rémi's camera. He's found me with his enormous telephoto lens, and he crouches discreetly at some distance away, capturing the closest thing he's had yet to a Real Me. Perhaps he realizes that I'm not trying to be anything for anyone now, which has otherwise been my biggest chore in life, bigger than paddling a river 600 miles, certainly, or doing anything else. When I give up the burden of trying to please others—a number one priority for my life these days—I become someone who secretes herself away from the world, reveling in anonymity.

CHAPTER TEN

‿‿⁊

I CAMPED WITH RÉMI LAST NIGHT, AND NOW HE CONTINUES UP THE river, leaving me with instructions to meet him at a village called Barga. The village lies at the place where the Niger enters giant Lake Debo, a convenient spot for him to get pictures of me crossing the lake. I've been dreading this crossing, just as Park must have dreaded it centuries before. In many ways, it is the most treacherous part of the journey as it takes an entire day to cross, and is so large that it's like traveling over an inland sea. Getting lost in the middle of it is a major concern. And then if a storm should catch me, overturning and separating me from my boat, the nearest land would be many miles in any direction, and there's a chance I could drown.

In the hopes of alleviating this possibility, the captain of Rémi's boat has urged me to follow their route across the lake. Without such guidance, I could literally get disoriented in the vast waters, having no sense of where the Niger begins again. It's a warning I take seriously, and so I agreed to meet them at Barga, spend the night there, and then proceed across the lake in their wake.

Given this plan, today's travel sounds delightfully straightforward and easy: I keep going until I reach Barga, a mere four to six hours of paddling away (according to Rémi's captain), and then I spend the remainder of the day resting at the village and preparing myself for the all-day crossing of Debo the following morning.

I love when things are straightforward and easy. Still, I know the Niger hates plans, and so I'm apprehensive of what sounds too good to be true. But I paddle along with my spirits raised: Lake Debo, no more than six hours away. Rain comes—inevitably—soaking me and my things, but it's a timid storm with no wind. I like these kinds of storms the most, as clouds block out the intense heat of the sun and the rain cools me off. The air has a gentle smell of verdant fields, heavy raindrops hitting the placid spread of water and sending out circular ripples.

Gradually, the storm passes and the sun starts to reappear, its reflection on the water blinding me. The heat returns, my thermometer reading 96 degrees and climbing. I paddle with barely a pause. Noon comes. Goes. And now one o'clock. Two. Three. No sight of an end to this river. No Lake Debo. No Barga.

I've been paddling for more than six hours now, and the river narrows to only 50 feet across—the narrowest it's been to date—but it doesn't seem to be going toward anything resembling an enormous lake. I put my hopes on each new bend in the river, assuring myself that I'll see Lake Debo finally. But the lake remains elusive, and I can see why Mungo Park was told that the Niger flows "to the end of the world."

I feel a clutch of panic when my watch reads four o'clock. I keep looking for Rémi's boat in the distance. Surely he knows that something is wrong by now, that it's been over six hours and I haven't appeared at Barga. But my anxiety is no good, it gets in the way, so I decide upon a new paddling strategy: I will simply accept my predicament. This works for a total of about fifteen glorious minutes, during which time I stop paddling to rest and eat a Snickers (my first meal since this morning), letting the speedy current carry me along. Mud banks rise high on either side, preventing any view of the surrounding countryside and creating a claustrophobic feel to my journey that I've not experienced before. But with my new strategy of being with what is, I just float along and rest my feet on the sides of my kayak, basking in the sun.

Up ahead, a man squats on the top of the bank, watching me. With the river so narrow, I can't avoid people even if I want to. I'm within earshot and eyeshot of everyone. As I float past, he stands and starts yelling at me, ordering me to come to him. I do the opposite: I paddle away. I feel like some child caught in the midst of a forbidden act, yet I have no idea what it is I've done. He runs after me along the top of the bank, shouting violently. No one owns the Niger; there aren't tariffs to pay for passing on it. (At least *that* much has changed since Mungo Park's time.) I can't think of a single reason why this man would be so fiercely angry at me, and I'm starting to get so curious about it that I slow down for a minute, let the panting man catch up.

He stops and yells out in broken French: "Give me 5,000 francs!" Which is the equivalent of about a week's worth of wages for your average Malian. And while I believe in charity, I don't believe in paying off yelling lunatics. He's literally jumping up and down now, repeating his demand and waving his hands. I find myself in a precarious position: I'm a woman traveling alone on a stretch of river where there's absolutely no one around, except some pissed-off guy trying to extort money from me. And what if I don't pay him? Will he come after me? Will he send runners to wait for me up ahead and ambush me on the river? Such things are possible—probably more possible than I think.

I decide to ignore the man and paddle as hard as I can. He runs after me for a while but finally gives up. So much for my 15 minutes of in-the-moment bliss. The fear is back, sitting like a bad meal in my gut. Every time the river curves, I look ahead for sight of men lying in wait for me in canoes, the river getting more and more narrow. I realize, but without surprise, that I've lived with constant fear on this trip. Fear of being chased, assaulted, robbed. Fear of bad weather and waves that might capsize my boat. Lots of fear. Fear of the wind, of harsh storms. Fear of hippos, crocodiles. Fear of being harassed by young men in passing boats, or of having my things stolen if I stop at villages. Endless fear. Fear of getting lost. Fear of not being able to find anyone if I do. All kinds of fear. My God. There's a large part of me that can't accept that a trip of mine isn't what you'd call "relaxing." There ought to be *something*, my mind reasons, that rises above all this unpleasantness.

The Niger abruptly branches in opposite directions. One branch heads northeast, the other west. A village of thatch and adobe huts sits at this juncture, and as my map of Mali is inaccurate and all but worthless, I consider going there to try to ask which route will get me to Lake Debo. The village people have noticed me, and they line up on the top of the riverbank to scream at me. No one responds to my greetings in Bambarra; they just holler and wave their arms, insisting that I paddle over to them and give them money. I wonder what it is about this stretch of the Niger. Why are folks so friendly and warm down by Ségou and so aggressive up here? What accounts for the change?

Park's guide, Amadi Fatouma, the sole survivor of his final journey, mentioned that their expedition encountered serious problems in the region of Lake Debo, then called "Sibby." Fatouma wrote: "In passing Sibby, three canoes came after us, armed with pikes, lances, bows and arrows, etc., but no firearms. Being sure of their hostile intentions, we ordered them to go back, but to no effect; and were obliged to repulse them by force." I have nothing with which to repulse anyone, except for some police-quality mace that I smuggled onto the plane from home. It's said to be effective on everything from human beings to grizzly bears, but I'm hoping I won't have to discover its real efficacy firsthand.

As my map is no help, I decide to simply pick a direction. I have a fifty-fifty chance of screwing up, which isn't the worst odds I've ever faced. I choose: west. The people in the village scream at me as I go by, and they don't stop screaming until I make it around a bend. Incredibly, the Niger, once a mile wide by Ségou, is now barely 30-feet across. I see no sign of civilization, which stumps me. If there's a big lake ahead, and a village called Barga, there must be other villages, too. And certainly there must be canoes or boats heading to those villages— which is the strangest, most unsettling aspect of this entire experience. *Where are the boats?*

None of it makes sense, and as the sun is now setting, I'm starting to panic. The villages—what few there are in these parts—all seem to be hostile. I contemplate camping alone on the top of one of these mud banks, in full view of anyone who wants money or anything else from me. And if I can manage to make it safely through the night, I'll still have no way of knowing if I'm heading toward Lake Debo in the morning.

I try to think about my predicament as reasonably as I can. It seems that the best thing to do would be to stop and ask someone where Lake Debo and Barga are. But I have to be careful who I ask. I paddle along, hoping to run into someone who might be willing to assist me. And now I hear the distant sound of women's voices floating down from the riverbank.

I try to find a place to pull over. I see a fissure in the high clay bank and manage to lodge my kayak in it. Pulling and clawing my way up the muddy slope to the ground above, I see before me a vast green expanse, a floodplain, which surely proves the presence of a nearby lake. Yet, I can't see the lake. In the distance are two small thatch huts, a couple of women standing before them and chattering to each other.

I wipe the mud from my arms, straighten my hat on my head, and walk toward them. They keep chattering away, not seeing me. One woman, unclothed from the waist up, perfectly round breasts exposed, pounds millet in a stone mortar. Her friend sits nearby, nursing a baby in her lap. A young girl, entirely naked but for a gold band in each ear, spots me before the adults do and lets out a cry that could signal the end of the world.

"*Tu-bab! Tuuuu-baaaab!*"

The women look up, astounded by the sight of me. They stop what they're doing, tattooed mouths hanging open. I might be some kind of apparition, come back from the dead. They look petrified with fear and wonder.

The little girl is still screaming and crying in terror: "*Tuubaab! Tuuu-baaab!*"

I smile and greet the women in my best Bambarra. "Hello," I say. "How is your family?"

They don't move.

"*Barga be mi?*" I ask. Where's Barga?

The woman nursing the baby bursts out laughing and repeats what I said, her eyes linked to mine.

I ask it again—"Where's Barga?"

She repeats my words again, saying them exactly as I had, imitating the poor pronunciation. The woman holding the pestle looks at me wild-eyed now, and violently slams it into the mortar. Again and again, she slams it down. Her large biceps quiver.

I consult my meager list of Bambarra words and phrases, written on the back of my notebook.

"What is the name of this village?" I ask, as clearly as possible.

"*Tuu-bab! Tuuuuu-bab!*" the little girl wails.

The nursing woman repeats what I say, laughing. I seem to be getting nowhere with them, though I can't figure out why. Surely they still speak Bambarra in these parts.

"Where's Lake Debo?" I try.

"Ai-eee!" the woman with the pestle yells, slamming it down with a head-crushing *whomp.*

"Is Lake Debo over there?" I ask.

"Ai-eee!" she screams.

"Uh," I say. "Well, it was nice meeting you all."

I turn around and quickly head back to the river, the woman still slamming her pestle down with ferocious zeal. "Ai-eee!" she calls after me. "Ai-eee!"

I wonder if this day can get any worse. I slide down the mud slope and free my kayak's rudder from where it's stuck in the clay. Getting inside, I start to paddle off. Just as the strong current takes hold of me, the two women call after me. They're standing on the top of the bank now. I crane my neck to hear what they're saying. Directions to Barga? Information about Lake Debo?

Then I hear them: "*Tubab—argent!*" White person—give us money!

⌣

I'VE BEEN PADDLING FOR NEARLY NINE HOURS NOW, VIRTUALLY nonstop, for a destination that should have arrived hours earlier. I still have no idea if I'm going in the right direction to meet up with

Rémi. Only the fast current is encouraging, helping me travel quickly for the first time during my trip.

The river curves and bends, and I see it broadening up ahead. A village! Many villages, all in a row, up and down the shore on both sides. Could the elusive Barga be one of them? But I don't see Rémi's boat parked anywhere. And there's no lake.

As I paddle past the shore, scores of people come running from thatch huts to watch me go by.

"Where's Barga?" I ask them in Bambarra and French.

No one seems to know what I'm talking about. They just stare and assail me with the ubiquitous calls for money. I look for men on shore, repeating my question to them as they're likely to be the educated ones and might know some French beyond the words for "money" and "give me." I ask every man I meet where Barga and Lake Debo are, but they shake their heads.

I slow down by one village, where a young man entreats me to repeat my question. There's something reassuring about his eyes, his demeanor, and he has excellent French. I ignore my fear of stopping at these villages and pull over.

He tells me his name is Aboka, though he prefers being called "Le Boss." From the cows grazing all around him, I assume he's Fulani. He scolds a crowd of kids nearby, telling them to be quiet and leave me alone so he can hear me. When he learns that I'm American, he smiles broadly.

"I study English in Bamako," he says. "Peace Corps teach me."

I'm thinking, thank God for the Peace Corps.

"I need to find Barga," I say slowly, enunciating the words.

"Barga? Yes. Over there." He points down the river, to where it branches again. He points to the branch going to the left. "Barga is at the end."

I ask him where the lake is, and he assures me that I'm very close, that Barga is on a small island where the river ends and the lake begins.

The sun sits on the horizon now, dropping behind evening mists. Time always seems to pass most speedily at the very end of the day, the sun scampering for cover. I thank Le Boss and leave him, paddling quickly down the left river channel, which is only an incredible 20 feet across, the current refreshingly fast and doing most of the work. At last, after coming round a small bend, I face the giant Lake Debo. It's like coming upon a vast ocean. All I see is water on all sides—water that reaches to the very end of the wide horizon before me—smack in the middle of the South Sahara. I can hardly believe it.

And Barga now, directly ahead. The teeming village of round, squat thatch huts rests on a narrow island at the mouth of the Niger.

I start making my way over, and people catch sight of me. In a matter of moments, the village is in an uproar. An enormous crowd collects onshore, watching, gesturing to me, demanding money. I don't see Rémi's boat anywhere, although it is so large it's usually hard to miss. I search the lake for sight of him, but I see no one. He should have arrived here many hours ago. I pull up to the island and dig my paddle into the mud to hold my kayak steady. Before I can do anything, the crowd descends upon me, trying to pull my backpack and dry bags from the kayak. The crowd is so thick that I can't move. Hands pull and clutch at my clothes, my body. Everything I own, including myself, is up for grabs.

"Whoa!" I yell. "Back off!"

The people are momentarily startled. I raise my paddle and grab back my bags. I can feel the adrenaline coursing through me.

Someone suddenly steps forward with a large stick and threatens the crowd with it. This man speaks some French, and I ask him if he's seen a Frenchman in a large pinasse.

"No," he says. "I don't see them. But you must ask the chief."

I don't want to ask the chief, not if it means getting out of the boat and leaving my stuff here, unguarded. When I tell him that, he calls over his friend, a man with ripped T-shirt and muddy pants, and orders him to fend off the onlookers while I'm gone. This man nods and steps into the water, hovering over my kayak. He swings a large stick menacingly at anyone who comes near.

"Lovely," I say, watching this.

I can relate to poor Mungo Park on his final journey: he absolutely refused to stop anywhere or get out of the boat. And here I am onshore, breaking Park's cardinal rule. The crowd is close against me again, barely allowing me to move. A zillion hands pinch, squeeze, poke me from all sides as I follow the guy with the French. I'm so exhausted from paddling all day with very little in my stomach, am so on edge from the crowd all around me and the futile search for Rémi, that I feel on the verge of losing whatever is left of my patience and sanity. I feel hot-wired, about to blow.

The current of the crowd carries me to the middle of the village. Thatch huts overrun all available space on the tiny island, the muddy, trampled ground showing no patches of green. The air holds an omnipresent smell of human urine and animal dung. The crowd stops me before a large thatch hut, and a man comes out to greet me. He's older, his hair showing traces of gray. He smiles at me in a strange, almost lascivious sort of way. When he shakes my hand, he won't let go of it, so that I'm forced to pull my fingers from his.

I greet him in Bambarra and get straight to the point, wanting to return to my kayak as soon as possible. I ask him if he's seen two tubab in a large boat. A man and a woman. The man is French, his name is Rémi. The woman, Heather, is an American.

"Where are you from?" the man asks, as if he never heard my question.

"The U.S.," I say. "Have you seen this Frenchman?"

"You are from America? What is your name?"

I tell him. I tell him my first and last names. At his insistence, I pull out my notebook and write it out for him.

"Ki-ra," he says, reading the letters.

"Yeah." I ask him again if he's seen Rémi.

"Are you married?" he replies.

I can feel my patience fizzling. "Please." I entreat him with my eyes. "Will you tell me if you've seen these two people?" Which shouldn't be hard to answer—they're probably the only white people to have set foot in Barga in the last *year*.

"What are their names?"

Though I have already given him their names, I give them to him again. He asks me to write them down for him, so I do. I write down "Rémi" and "Heather" in big letters. He needs help pronouncing Heather's name, and it takes him several tries to say it correctly. I feel like a TESL instructor.

"Do you have a boyfriend?" he asks.

I sigh. I scan the shore of the island, looking for Rémi's big boat, seeing nothing.

The chief repeats Heather's name a couple of times again, then looks up at me. "I haven't seen them," he announces.

"All righty," I say. "Thank you." I turn around and head back to my kayak, pushing through the current of bodies as if wading upstream.

"Madame! Madame!" The chief chases after me and grabs my arm. He looks excited.

"Yes?"

"Money, madame." He smiles and shrugs.

I fish into my pocket and pull out a bill, dropping it into his palm. Other men in the crowd rush forward. "*L'argent, Madame! Madame!*

Madame! L'argent!" They press against me, holding on to my arms.

I was afraid of this, that the minute I went passing out money the crowd would go nuts. But I, too, am going nuts. I know that nothing can hold back my temper now. I know that in a matter of moments I'm going to be completely out of control. I try to escape to my boat, but the hands still hold me back. All at once, I lose it. My elbows fly out and my arms are swinging against the hands that hold me. People step away, alarmed, and I break through the crowd, pushing aside bodies, my steps not faltering for anyone.

"*Pardon! Pardon!*" I yell out, flying through the crowd. Startled people back up, allowing me passage to my boat.

The man with the torn T-shirt and large stick is still there, fending off the crowd. I give him some money for his assistance, and he smiles, touches the bills to his forehead, and waves his club with renewed vigor. Everything about this scene is absolutely surreal. I glance to see if my things are where I left them in the kayak, then I press them down, securing them. Picking up my paddle, I pull my boat into the water and get in. The crowd makes one final grab for the kayak, and my protector jumps forward, grimacing at the people and yelling until they let go. I paddle off quickly into the dusk, traveling against the current and back up the Niger, the crowd shouting after me.

I head to Le Boss's Fulani village, figuring it's my best bet for security tonight. The current is so strong that I crawl up the river, inch by inch. I wouldn't be able to do such strenuous paddling were it not for all the wild energy that still rushes out of me. I paddle furiously, wondering where Rémi is. Does he know how hard it is to locate him when I'm paddling alone in a kayak in the middle of West Africa, people freaking out on me? The hell with the pictures he wants of me crossing Lake Debo. The hell with all that bullshit. I'll just hire some local person to show me the route across the lake tomorrow.

I finally reach Le Boss's village, called Guro. I pull my kayak onto the bank, my clothes drenched with sweat, my body shaking. Le Boss comes to the bank and greets me. He says he's glad I came back, and he encourages me to eat dinner with his parents and spend the night here. I thank him, amazed by the difference between villages barely a mile apart: Barga's madness compared to Guro's blessed sanity. I've no sooner tied up my kayak than Le Boss hands me a calabash full of warm, foaming, freshly drawn cow's milk.

"Please, just sit for a moment," he says to me, concern in his eyes. "Drink and rest, okay?"

I do as he tells me. I sit down on the riverbank and drink the cow's milk. No crowds surround me in this village. No one asks for money. Le Boss brings some of his younger brothers over to help unload my backpack and dry bags from the kayak, then the boys return to carry the kayak itself into the village. I sit with my knees up, head resting on them, observing my quivering hands. I feel the familiar up and down movements of river waves, as if I were still paddling on the Niger. I shudder at the thought of passing Barga again tomorrow.

I finish the milk, and Le Boss leads me to the village. Cows graze between the thatch huts, staring at me like sentinels as I pass. I go to meet his parents. His aging father, Hamaduna Ba, sits regally on a mat in a blue grand bubu shirt, inviting me to take a seat beside him. He's married to three wives, who busily prepare a meal for all of us. I give Hamaduna some money as a gift and thank him for his hospitality. He shakes his head deferentially.

"It is my pleasure," he says in perfect French. "Perhaps you'd like to change into dry clothes?"

"Yes," I say.

He has a son carry my backpack into his thatch hut, and Hamaduna himself pulls a mat over the door to give me privacy. It smells warm and soft inside, like dry hay, the family's few possessions—clothes, a storage chest, a stool—lined up neatly against the far side of the dwelling. I shed my wet clothes, enjoying the luxury of putting dry ones over my skin.

Hamaduna waits for me outside with special Malian tea prepared, and I join him on the mat again. It's a thick mint tea, syrupy and sweet. Per the Malian custom, I completely finish my glass and pass it along to Le Boss to drink from. Together, we watch the sun go down, night settling around us. Hamaduna tells me that he recently went to Paris for his 50th birthday. He and his first wife stayed in a fancy hotel and drank Bordeaux and rode the Metro. I try to imagine this man beside me, sitting before a hut made from woven thatch, cows gathered all around him like minions, riding the Paris subway. But Hamaduna is a wealthy man by Malian standards; he tells me his cows are worth about $380 apiece. And he has a herd of nearly 100, with an additional 25 calves.

"Do you eat chicken?" he asks me.

I tell him I do, so Hamaduna sends the kids running after some birds.

Hamaduna asks what brings me here. When I explain that I was supposed to meet some friends at Barga who never showed up, he asks for further details—how many people, what kind of boat—and then passes on the information to a couple of his sons. The boys leave in canoes, going to the different villages in the area to ask if anyone has seen Rémi. I'm dazed by Hamaduna's generosity and assistance. It is as Park discovered 200 years before: no two villages in Mali are alike, and nothing is predictable.

While I am talking to Hamaduna and Le Boss, one of Hamaduna's sons runs over to tell me he's seen Rémi's boat on the river nearby. The captain of the boat is shining a spotlight in the darkness, trying to find me. I go to the shore, and sure enough, there's Rémi's boat. He's calling out to me.

I wonder what happened. Did he take another branch of the Niger? Did he encounter trouble somewhere? Was he searching for me on Lake Debo?

I call to him, and he stands on the side of the boat to greet me. The barge brushes up against the shore, stopping, and he jumps onto the ground.

"Hello!" he says.

"I was at Barga, asking around, but I didn't see you," I say in a rush. "The people said you never came. I didn't know what to do."

"I was on that hill. You see? Over there." He points to the east, to a distant, high hill, its top outlined in the moonlight. "Kira, it was so beautiful. I climbed the hill and I was taking pictures from the top. Ah, it was incredible! The sun was setting.... It was perfect." He sputters his lips and shakes his head. "*Parfait.*"

CHAPTER ELEVEN

～

LAKE DEBO TODAY. THE WEATHER WILL MEAN EVERYTHING. I WAKE UP early and lie in my tent, nervous about the crossing. The sun hasn't risen yet and it's gray out, so I can't tell if a storm is coming. And even if there isn't one now, one could come later in the day. Hamaduna told me that if a storm hits while I'm in the middle of Lake Debo, the waves can be dangerously large. I remember seeing the lake last night: just a sheet of water as far as the eye can see. No land, nothing until I get to the other side. Half the challenge of crossing Debo lies in the fact that I must complete the journey in a single day; there can be no stopping if I get tired, no dallying.

The cows of Guro gather around my tent, chewing on grass and staring at me. I sit up, my whole body aching as if I'd spent all of yesterday climbing up a mountain. *Up a river*, I think. I get out of the tent and take it down. Guro would be quiet were it not for the roosters' head-splitting calls waking up the humans. I'll need to wait for Rémi to get up. I walk over to a calf tied to a post and scratch its neck. It stretches out its forelegs like a dog and wags its tail, letting out satisfied *humphs*.

To the west, across a green flood plain, I can see Lake Debo covered with morning mists.

I wonder what troubles Park had when he crossed it. According to his guide, Fatouma, the group was attacked on the lake, but nothing more is known. Still, Park made it across somehow, and the thought of his success renews my feeling of determination.

Le Boss emerges from a nearby hut and waves to me.

"Kira," he yells, looking at me petting the calf, "you can buy that cow and take it back to America with you!"

"It'd be hard to get on the plane."

"I'll sell it to you for cheap."

"I don't think the National Geographic Society would pay for it."

Rémi and Heather are getting out of their tent nearby. They head onto the boat for some Earl Grey and rich tea biscuits, their Malian cook coming over to take down their tent. The roosters are finally shutting up, strutting between the huts and jerking their heads. I carry my backpack to the shore and secure it inside my kayak, being careful about weight distribution. If the weight is even slightly greater on one side, my kayak's nose will veer off in that direction—not unlike a car with poor wheel alignment. What this means in terms of a full day of paddling is that one arm will have to work harder than the other to keep the kayak straight.

I sit on the shore, eating a Snickers bar for breakfast. Seeing this, Rémi comes over to invite me to breakfast in his boat, and I walk the gangplank to join them. Forgetting my manners, I heap sugar and cream into my cup of tea, wanting to get as many calories into me as possible. Rémi and Heather encourage me to help myself to the biscuits, which I do. I plough through the package. Meanwhile, we chat and joke about stuff, and I'm glad for their company and this diversion, as it helps calm my nerves about the paddling. Part of me wants to delay what I know will be a hot, grueling crossing. The sun already burns over the water from the east, melting the newly applied sunscreen from my face. Another hot one. No doubt about it.

I finish up and leave the boat to say goodbye to Le Boss and his father. I get in my kayak, the whole family standing on the shore to wish me a safe journey. The current sweeps me toward Barga, with Rémi's boat puttering past.

At this time of day, Barga looks sleepy. The narrow Niger expels me into huge Lake Debo, and I pass the island village without drawing much of a crowd. Rémi's boat motors ahead of me, trailing back and forth as he takes photos of my paddling. I feel as if I'm in a *Sports Illustrated* photo shoot now, so I do my best to look Athletic, though my tired arms and upper body don't feel like cooperating today. What I need is a few days of downtime, which I don't anticipating having until—or unless—I get to Timbuktu.

It's not long before the horizon shows only a meeting of sky and water on all sides of me, the waves sizable and unruly. I've read that this part of the lake is 160 feet deep, which makes my crossing feel all the more hazardous. If I were to overturn, lose my things, there would be little hope of recovering them. But perhaps there is something to be said for a Dogon witch's assistance, because there's still not a single cloud in the sky and no hint of a rising storm. Such a day is a total fluke at this time of year, wind and rain the norm.

Rémi's boat leaves me behind, becoming a small brown dot on the horizon up ahead. I keep following that dot. A river steamer passes me, so loaded with people and baggage that the water nearly overtakes the gunwales. The ship overshadows me like a giant, her crew cheering and howling, the passengers craning to get a look at me, this woman in her tiny red boat, paddling feverishly beside their swift passage.

I'm starting to find this crossing rather intimidating. Without landmarks to reach, it can seem, in the midst of such a great spread of water, that I don't go anywhere. I have to keep reminding myself that I still make progress. As long as I keep paddling, I can be confident I'll get somewhere. Before long, I see white buoys in the distance, meant to guide boats to where the Niger picks up again. I reach one buoy and then the next, all sight of land gone and Rémi's boat a speck to the northwest now. The heat starts to become intense, my thermometer reading 106 degrees. The hottest day yet. But there can be no stopping.

I catch up with Rémi finally, where his boat is tied to a buoy. I grab hold of the side, taking the opportunity to rest for a few minutes and drink some water. I see a sandbar rising in the distance, proof of how shallow Debo can be in spots, the rainy season coming later and later in recent years, drying the lake up and encouraging the Sahara to encroach farther south.

My crossing becomes straightforward now: I just follow the buoys. Which is a relief. Still, Rémi waits for me at intervals so that I have a chance to rest by his boat every half hour or so. Heather cheers me at each leg of the journey, which really helps to make the crossing more pleasant, even with all the heat and incessant paddling.

More islands start to rise from the lake, and soon I'm entering a wide channel, heading toward land and the mouth of the Niger. Hippos peer at me from the shallows—the first hippos I've seen—their heads rising and lowering, air spraying from their nostrils. Lake Debo, the part I'd worried about most, barely stirs behind me.

I decide to stop off in the first village after Debo, a town called Aka, to see if they have any mangoes or other supplies to sell, as my food stocks are getting low. The kids of the village see me coming and crowd onshore, shouting and pointing. It's the largest concentration of kids I've seen to date, and I hope things will go more smoothly than at previous villages.

As I near the shore, the kids swim into the river en masse to check out my kayak. This has never happened before—usually when I'm in the water, I'm safe. Before I can paddle to deeper water, the crowd surrounds me and threatens to push me out of my boat. Kids are everywhere, trying to climb into my kayak or pull it to shore. I decide to humor everyone this time. I pick up a little girl to lift her into the kayak, but the minute my hands touch her she screams and stiffens all her limbs, refusing to get inside. Another girl volunteers, but when I touch her, she screeches as if in pain. There is obviously something terrifying about being touched by a tubab, though I can't figure out what.

Now a boy steps forward—a remarkably brave boy, given the risks of a white person's touch—and he actually tries to pull himself inside my kayak. I lift him up and put him inside, and his friends look on with fear and wonder as he makes himself comfortable in front of me and waves at them. *This boy*, I'm thinking, *is destined for greatness.*

We go for a ride together, and now his face of confidence and equanimity breaks into a look of terror as the kayak wobbles back and forth. He hollers and braces himself with his hands, as if riding on a roller coaster for the first time, but quickly calms himself and regains his composure. The kids all yell and cheer him on, and when he's at last sure he won't fall out, he raises a fist of victory like Muhammad Ali.

I deposit him beside his friends again, and they all slap him on the back and crowd around him. They shoot out questions, as if he'd just returned from the dead. It turns out that Aka doesn't have any food to sell, so I turn my kayak around and paddle on toward Timbuktu.

⌣

It's been one of those strange days on the river. I spent the entire time paddling but seemed to make no progress. The river curved and dipped but got me nowhere, and half the time I was fighting against the wind. I'm beat and nearly out of food, and with the sun going down, I approach a prosperous-looking village to try to buy a meal and lodging for the night. Stopping at villages is always a crapshoot. What tribe will I get? Will they have food to sell me? Will they like me?

I'm greeted by the usual crowd of 50-plus people, naked kids swarming around me and yelling excitedly. They tell me that this large collection of adobe huts is called Berakousi and that it lies at the spot where the Koula River enters the Niger. I see goats nearby; women pound millet. I ask what people this is and am told they're Bozo.

As I go in search of the chief, it quickly becomes evident that they don't want me here. Young toughs, one sporting a black T-shirt with Osama bin Laden's face printed on it like a rock star's, start harassing me in pathetic French. Where's my husband? Would I like to have sex with them? What man back home allowed me to travel here by myself? Their faces are covered with indigo head-wraps, in the manner of North African Tuaregs, just their eyes peering out at me. Obviously, it's cool to look Tuareg here. I ignore them, nearly being knocked to my feet by the crowd of pushy onlookers as I try to move forward. I've noticed a fine but palpable division between curiosity and aggression toward outsiders along the Niger, and Berakousi village clearly crosses the line. I don't want to stay here. But food is important, so I need to find the chief.

He's out in the fields, so I sit on a wicker chair to wait for him. I refuse numerous requests from women who keep trying to pass me their babies, wanting me to breastfeed them. The sun is fast departing, and I'm worried now, because the river's too choppy and mercurial along this stretch to make night paddling safe, and I didn't see an alternative village nearby.

Finally, the chief appears, an old man named Gardja Jemai, who walks over and surveys me, frowning. I give him a large sum of money as cadeau, explain as best I can that I'd like to buy a meal if possible. And if he can't spare any food, I'll just be on my way. He stands there, frowning, saying nothing. I pass money to the best French speaker in the crowd and ask him to translate my request. There is a brief exchange and I'm told to wait.

I wait, and wait. The sun, I notice, is nearly gone. Too late to go else-where. The village people continue to crowd around me. I sigh and try to resign myself to the situation, asking the chief if I can sleep on a patch of ground nearby. He holds out his hand for more money, and when I give him a wad of bills, he nods. The young men sit around me, demanding money, too. One guy tells me that he wants the watch and flashlight that I've just taken out of my backpack. He picks up these things and fingers them. Meanwhile, I am the subject of a large, com-munal conversation, my title *tubabu*—"whitey"—being exchanged excitedly by members of the crowd.

A woman, one of the chief's four wives, comes over and announces that she has food for me. I thank her and give her some money, and she drops a bowl in front of me. Inside sits a rotting fish head, blooms of fungus growing on its skin.

"*Mangez*," the woman says. She puts her fingers to her lips.

And I'm so hungry and fatigued that I do. I just don't care anymore. I crack open the mottled fish skin and pull out bits of white meat. Everyone laughs heartily, and I see that this is a joke, feeding me a dog's dinner. When I finish, I notice that Osama and Co. have requisi-tioned one of my pens. I decide to just let it go, hoping that the situa-tion won't escalate. I recall a grim passage from Park's narrative, about his Moorish captors: "They had recourse to the final and deci-sive argument, that I was a Christian, and of course that my property was lawful plunder…. They accordingly opened my bundles, and robbed me of everything they fancied." The young men nudge me, speak threateningly to me through their Tuareg face-wrappings, the chief—traditionally my benefactor—standing by and doing nothing. When one man puts his hand around my wrist, I wrench my arm away, holding up a fist.

"Don't touch me," I say.

The village people laugh. I get up, scolding myself for my loss of temper, scolding the fear within me that caused it. I put on my backpack, heading to the shore. Can I still get out of here tonight? But it's darkness all around, the Niger churning madly before the confluence of the Koula River. I'm stuck. Nothing to be done.

I wish I didn't feel such fear and anger now. But I do. Those emotions stay. My time in this village tonight, with the young men taunting me, feels like a miniature production of larger world events. Fear begetting fear. People feeling threatened, alienated, enraged. Not wanting to provoke anyone, or to be further provoked, I sit for hours on the dark shore, slapping mosquitoes, hoping that the people in the village will get bored waiting for me and go back to their huts. It feels like a true Mungo Park moment: "I felt myself as if left lonely and friendless amidst the wilds of Africa," he wrote in one of his last journal entries. Yes.

When I finally return, the village has cleared out, and one of the chief's wives smiles in pity, bringing out a foam mattress for me to sleep on. I lie down and wrap myself in my tent's rain fly, my clothes becoming soaked with sweat. Fleas and other assorted insects crawl up my legs, up my clothes, get caught in my hair. They bite me incessantly. My chest burns, and I shine a flashlight down my shirt, seeing my breasts covered with bites. I slather on 100 percent DEET bug repellent, the stuff that melts plastic. I don't even care. I shut my eyes to wait for first light, when I'll leave this place. It is one of those nights that I know I must get through, that promises no sleep.

~⌁

I ESCAPE FROM BERAKOUSI IN THE FIRST LIGHT OF DAWN, JUST AS THE roosters crow out their ear-popping paeans to the morning. It was Mungo Park's same strategy—to leave before any of his tormentors had a chance to wake up. ("Early in the morning," he wrote, "before the Moors were assembled, I departed.") I've learned a lot from Mungo about how to do this trip. More than simply teaching me how to greet village elders, handle crowds, and escape from unpleasant villages, he emphasized the importance of patience and acceptance of whatever comes, no matter how difficult the events.

Being as silent as possible, I stuff my tent fly into my backpack and slip it on, grabbing my paddle. The village slumbers, except for a couple of women who fetch water from the Niger. It's too dark to see if any of my things have been pinched during the night, though I doubt it: I was awake nearly the whole time. I have that heavy, sunken feeling that no sleep gives me, as if my body were functioning on slow-speed. This state has allowed a mix of dark emotions to rise to the surface of my mind, leaving me feeling absolutely defenseless before them. There is depression that I chose to do a trip that has proved so exhausting and difficult. Disappointment over getting so angry in the village last night. Despair at how much farther I have to go, through the storms and heat and increasingly hostile country.

I try to push all the emotions away. It's my only option, given where I am, given the circumstances. I must suppress everything into blissful apathy. And after a few moments, I succeed. With a feeling akin to indifference, I watch the waves of the Niger slapping the shore and reaching out to me. I put my backpack into the kayak. Getting in, I paddle hard, leaving Berakousi far behind me.

If I'm learning anything on this journey, it still feels shady and inconclusive. But I do know that a lesson repeats itself every time a fisherman passes in his canoe, not bothering to return my greeting, just asking for money or gifts. People don't seem interested in me much beyond what I might be able to give them. They see my white skin and reduce me to an identity I can't shake: Rich White Woman, Bearer of Gifts, nothing more. This is an important lesson—the way people so easily label and dismiss each other. I'm dismayed by how simple it is for me to get caught in the same game, to start seeing every passing man in a canoe as a threat or as someone who only wants something from me. In this cordoning off of the people I meet, in this mistrust, I deny them their humanity. Do we ever greet people without wanting something from them? Without hoping they'll give us certain things in return—love, money, approval? Without wanting them to change, or to do what we want, or to see us the way we want to be seen? What's stopping us from simply finding joy in another's presence? I'm miffed by it all.

My stomach grumbles from no breakfast, but I keep paddling north, into the great bend of the Niger that does a 180-degree turn through the South Sahara on its approach to the town of Niafounké. Whenever the river curves, winds tend to blow directly at me. This stretch is no exception, a fierce wind striking my face, sending large waves against me, the current trying to pull my kayak toward shore. Attempting to paddle into such strong winds and giant swells feels futile, but the alternative is to wait around all day, hoping for a respite from the weather, which means making no progress whatsoever. And because this is the rainy season, the longer in the day I wait, the more susceptible I am to late afternoon storms. So I paddle hard to stay on course, my arms crying out in pain, though I've taught myself to ignore it. None of this is fun or challenging or exciting—it just is. I take whatever comes, my body too busy with paddling to give my mind a chance to protest.

No one is out in this kind of weather. That's one thing I've learned about river travel on the Niger: if the locals are out in their canoes, it's safe to paddle. These people have been fishermen for millennia, and they know a bad day when they see one. Still, I don't wait for good days as they do; I want to know that with every minute that passes, I'm getting closer to Timbuktu. I travel from landmark to landmark, hoping as I edge around each bend that the wind will shift behind me and offer me its assistance. But as the hours go by, I'm still fighting this river. My concentration stays fixed on the large whitecaps that strike my kayak from the side and try to flip me over.

At midday, opposite a sizable village, I pull over to take a rest. My arms are smarting, and I haven't eaten anything since the rotting fish head the night before. I burn so many calories from the constant, hard paddling all day that I'm perpetually hungry. I search deep in my backpack for some forgotten food and am rewarded for my efforts: a smashed Snickers. It feels like a gift from the gods. I sit down to eat it, only now noticing how the current carries over raw sewage from the village across the river and deposits it up and down the shore—human shit everywhere, congealing in the sun. But with the apathy still left over from earlier this morning, I don't care. The villages along the Niger have their own wells for drinking water; everyone knows not to drink from the polluted Niger, the river acting as washing place and communal toilet for thousands—if not millions—of people by the time it reaches its termination in Nigeria.

As I eat, a canoe passes close to the shore with a couple of families inside. I wave to everyone and say hello in Songhai, the new lingua franca of these parts. Men standing on either end of the canoe, poling it along, yell out, "*Cadeau, madame! Cadeau!*" They hold out their hands for money. The kids start taking up the chorus: "*Cadeau, madame! Cadeau! Cadeau!*"

I look down at my feet until they pass.

CHAPTER TWELVE

~

FOR THE FIRST TIME, IT FEELS AS IF TIMBUKTU IS GETTING CLOSE. Perhaps it's the sight of large dunes bordering the river, or maybe it's the heat that grows each day, well over 100 degrees. But the desert country has arrived, almost unnoticed, slowly altering the landscape with each mile traveled, making it drier, thirstier for the waters of the Niger. I don't see anything green anymore, as I had at the start of my trip. No jungle-like views along the river. No trees except for the rare ones planted in a village. Another day ends in this scorching country, the sun low to the west and the light getting soft. I remind myself that I've been paddling for weeks already. No one to really converse with to help me pass the time. No major diversions until the very end of each day, when I pull over at the nearest village, never knowing what's going to happen.

Before my trip, it had seemed daunting, the idea of being alone on this river for so long, with nothing to do but paddle. But I've grown used to it by now. The West, with all its rush and stress, has trained me to believe that I must fill every moment of every day with something "important." What counts as "important," though, is never entirely clear. I know that spending weeks paddling a kayak on the Niger would *not* have been important by my former criteria. In fact, the idea would have been an all-out affront to that old frame of mind. Paddling doesn't seem worthy enough, somehow, or practical, or sensible enough. It seems like an abhorrent waste of time. But what would I be doing instead? I smile at the answer: finishing my Ph.D. in English. Writing dreary seminar papers. Reading countless books—volume after volume of stale critical theory written by people who are convinced they have the right answers. Listening to the endless lectures about so-and-so and such-and-such, with titles like "A Revolutionary Aim: Serialization and the Role of the Temperance in Delaney's *Blake*." Mulling over a dissertation "statement of intent," being told that all worthwhile endeavors have clear and definable objectives from the start. That all worthwhile endeavors must yield something tangible, something valuable, which furthers one's career or brings in money or achieves a certain standing. *These* are the things I would be doing instead, if I weren't on this river.

I laugh. I laugh loud enough to send some nearby birds squawking away. I see my life now as if it were all finished and laid out before me. I see the things I did in order to get somewhere, to do something else. I see the things that once mattered to me, and now don't. So much of it seems so strange and so silly and so tragic, all at once. All of it a way to bide time, a way to wait and plan and plot for the kind of life I wanted. But paddling on the Niger—now that is a real doing. For the first time, I feel as if I have no influence on the outcome. I just keep paddling, and this life of mine shows me what it thinks I should know. It tells me what it thinks is actually important.

Traveling as I am, slowly, deliberately, I memorize every nuance of this river. Every bend, every curve. The way the land seems to jut sharply from a distance, only to smooth out upon my approach. The persistence of the winds that are always carving and shaping the high white dunes, sending sand whirling into the Niger. As I've become entirely dependent on the weather and other natural conditions, I've learned to be acutely aware of my environment. I recognize the cause of various eddies, smell changes in wind and weather, feel the ever-so-subtle pull on my kayak's rudder that tells me how to best alter my course. I can tell the time from the position of the sun, am accurate nearly to the minute, though such accuracy has become unimportant. I no longer wear a watch, don't want one. When the sun goes down, I know it's time to pull over. That simple. And I take whatever I get. A friendly village, a hostile village. I take whatever comes.

I feel a new patience that requires no effort on my part. It results naturally from each day, from an understanding that no matter how hard I paddle, it makes little difference. Timbuktu stays far away, and these hours don't pass any faster. I have no obligations out here; my mind can't scold and cajole me into a new project. I'm not bothered by calls or e-mail or people at my door. Here, I have no choice but to be completely present in each moment of my life. Mali slowly, meticulously, imprints itself on my mind.

New, more basic concerns replace the old, tedious, programmed ones. For example, taking meals. I've learned to eat only when the sun reaches a certain spot in the sky and not before, regardless of my stomach's protests. To eat too much too often is to be wasteful and not ration what little food I have—which is almost nothing now, just some dried fruit and granola from home. Rationing takes self-discipline, though, and has been one of the hardest things I've had to teach myself. Not only do I refuse to eat food from my stocks more than twice a day, but the portion must be conservative—a handful of granola, say—as I can't rely on villages to have food to sell or dinner to offer, and I need enough to get me to Timbuktu.

There are also paddling concerns. I must try to get the majority of my paddling done before or after the midday hours, when the sun is hottest and the wind is strongest, both thwarting my progress. As I'm now well into the Sahel, the South Sahara, I'm also experiencing a different kind of weather during the rainy season from what prevailed down by Ségou. Here, violent storms arrive late in the afternoon or during the night, so that I need to paddle hard to find a secure place to sleep by the day's end.

Which brings up concerns about where to sleep. Do I camp or do I stay in a village? Before, I chose villages for greater safety, but lately this has seemed just as dangerous an option as camping alone along the Niger. Though I always pay the people I stay with, I don't want to go to a village where I'll be a burden to anyone, or where the people might feel hostility toward outsiders. But it's hard to know the status of a village when I'm simply paddling by and must go on appearances, so camping has become an attractive choice again—as long as I can find a remote place where no one will visit me, and I can get a good night's sleep.

Still, I prefer staying in villages and getting to know the people. Usually, I look for places with cows, which will probably be Fulani villages. For some reason, the Fulani have invariably been among the most welcoming of the peoples I've encountered. And their cows, of course, mean the possibility of milk to purchase. But lately I haven't seen many Fulani villages, so I look for other signs to help me choose. Generally, if people don't yell out requests for money or gifts as soon as I go by, that's a good sign. Even better if only a few kids run to shore. The less people react to my being an oddity, the more privacy I can usually expect to find. I try to avoid larger villages too, as huge crowds tend to overwhelm me in these places. My main concern is avoiding a repeat of my experience with the fish head and the young toughs in Berakousi.

I see that I have about an hour of light left, so I look for a place to pull over. I pass a fisherman heading back to his village and start up a conversation, inquiring how close I am to the large town of Niafounké.

"It's over there," he says in French, pointing to a distant bend in the Niger that would take nearly two hours to reach. Then he says, in a quiet, polite sort of way, "Money, miss?"

I slip him a bill. He asks where I'll be spending the night and when I shrug, he suggests his village. It seems to fit all my criteria: it's small, has no crowds, and there are some cows nearby. When I ask him if I can camp beside the village, he smiles and nods his head, encouraging me to come to shore. I follow him, tying up my kayak next to his long canoe. This village, he tells me, is named Dagougi; the people are Songhai. As women come to the shore to greet me, I see that they're unadorned but for gold earrings. Unlike the Fulani, they don't have any facial tattoos. They watch me set up my tent outside the village, donkeys wandering about and noisily cropping grass.

Dagougi sits on a hill overlooking the Niger. It's composed of neat, rectangular adobe homes, their backs facing out so that they form a large defensive square with a single entranceway. I began to notice this "fortification" layout shortly after I crossed Lake Debo, and it's a widespread characteristic of Upper Niger village architecture. Not so very long ago, people in these parts needed to keep themselves safe from desert marauders, such as Arabs coming from the north or tribes invading from farther south. Hence, their villages took on the form of mini-garrisons. The degree of fortification depends on the village, though I've passed places so completely surrounded by high adobe walls that I could see nothing inside but the tops of the minarets. Along the Upper Niger, the architecture speaks of a rich and often brutal history, empires vying with each other, entire villages living in fear of enslavement or slaughter.

The great Songhai empire reigned in these parts, off and on, from

A.D. 1100 to 1600, meeting with periods of defeat from the invading Tuareg or Malian empires. The German explorer Heinrich Barth, who made it across the Sahara to Timbuktu in 1853, would comment on the "excellent historical works" of the Songhai people, noting their strong place in the scholarship of the region and of Africa as a whole. The Songhai didn't enjoy true power here until their greatest leader, Ali the Great, expelled the Tuareg from Timbuktu in 1468. He then reigned for 28 years, conquering most of the country that I've paddled through and wresting the great commercial city of Djenné from the Malian empire of Bambarra. Ali was succeeded by his general, Askia the Great, who strengthened his empire's association with Islam and made a famous journey across the Sahara to Mecca. The experience greatly inspired him: he started a series of holy wars against neighboring tribes shortly after he returned, conquering as far east as present-day Niger and reaching as far west as the Atlantic Ocean. Before long, the Songhai ruled over a kingdom that extended a thousand miles east to west, enabling cities like Timbuktu to prosper as never before. It was this prosperity that Leo Africanus wrote about in his book *History and Description of Africa and the Notable Things Contained Therein* and that encouraged Europeans to reach Timbuktu.

∽

I PASS THE TOWN OF NIAFOUNKÉ EARLY THIS MORNING, THE NIGER starting to look more and more interminable. I figure it's the heat getting to me. My sunscreen doesn't really work anymore; I sweat so badly that I'm constantly wiping my face, and whatever remains rolls off with the perspiration. I put on my long-sleeved shirt, which makes things much hotter but protects my skin from the sun. Before me, the Niger goes on and on, beginning a long straight stretch. I've become a good judge of my paddling speed, and usually I can accurately estimate how long it will take me to get to a distant landmark. In this case, though, I don't even see a curve up ahead to act as a point of reference. Still, I must be getting closer to Timbuktu, and that's encouraging. I'm starting to believe I may actually make it, that this crazy trip of mine might actually be successful.

After a few hours of paddling, I reach the end of the straight stretch. The Niger curves to the east, splitting around an island. Rather than taking the longer, outside curve, I opt for a shortcut down the shallower channel. This is preferable, too, because I want to avoid passing the villages that border the other branch. The screaming, incessant calls for cadeaux have been getting much worse with each day that passes.

I paddle through what appears to be a kind of marshland, passing dark brown objects floating in the water. Used to seeing such fishermen's floats attached to underwater nets, I think nothing of them until one rises and spurts out air, two eyes peering at me: hippo! Hippos everywhere—I've never seen so many in one place. A whole hippo colony, and I'm stuck in the middle of it.

This is the worst of my nightmares. I've often debated what I would do if caught in such a situation, and I never had any good answers. During the first half of my trip, I didn't see hippos at all—most of them had been shot by locals, the teeth sold on the black market. But in this part of the Niger, for whatever reason, the hippos are flourishing.

All I know about hippos is what I've gleaned from PBS shows, that they're cute but bad-tempered critters whose skin produces a natural sunscreen. At night, they come on shore to forage, which is when you want to be sure you don't run into one. I've heard that hippos are more dangerous than lions, more vicious than crocodiles, and that they readily protect their young to the death. And I see baby hippos here.

Park noted the local people's fear of them: "We saw three hippopotami close to another of these islands. The canoe men were afraid they might follow us and upset the canoes. The report of a musket will in all cases frighten them away." It's all the advice I've received: try a loud noise.

"Nice hippos," I say to them. "Good hippos."

The hippos just watch me. My rubber boat would be no match for their teeth, yet they seem lazy enough, a mother and baby lounging nearby. I slowly turn my kayak around, and all at once I paddle in a fury against the current, back toward the other branch of the Niger. I paddle as if I were going through a minefield, trying to retrace my original route. Hippo heads rise as I pass, making sounds like whales as they shoot air from their nostrils. The dark eyes watch me from just above the surface of the water, assessing, granting me passage.

<hr />

As if hippos weren't bad enough, the Tonka rapids are coming. This is a natural aberration in the landscape, a strange rocky cleft that cuts through the sand of the South Sahara and enters the Niger, disturbing its course. The river flows in a tight S shape at this one spot, after millennia of trying to meander its way past the blockage. Boulders of black rock form a wall across the river, compressing it and speeding up its current; during Mali's colonial days, the French cleared a small passageway in the middle to allow the passage of river barges. But the boulders remain everywhere under the surface, threatening boats and tossing the waters; during bad weather the rapids can become nearly impassable.

I approach the middle of the wall of rock, paddling toward a buoy that marks the place for safe passage. Though the weather is relatively calm today, wind churns the water, creating swirling, tugging eddies that try to take over the maneuvering of my boat. The current reigns here, seizing my kayak and hurling me toward a rocky bend. I paddle hard to reach a sandy bank on the opposite shore, finally making it. I decide I'll wait for an approaching river barge to show me the best route across the final part of the rapids. Loaded with people and supplies, the boat travels slowly over the fierce eddies, skirting large black rocks that rise from the water. I paddle immediately in its wake, successfully passing the dangerous parts, until the river spurts me into a long straightaway. So much for the dreaded rapids of Tonka. Dunes rise on either side of the river, baking in the Saharan sun.

To my right, I see the familiar brown "floats" again, which I now know to be hippo heads. This time, though, I stay at a safe distance from them as I paddle in the middle of the river. A couple of boys in a canoe start spreading out a fishing net behind me, heading straight for them.

"*Hang-ya! Hang-ya!*" I say in Songhai to them. "Hippos!" I point at the creatures.

The boys glance to where I'm pointing, then look back at me and laugh. They put out the last of their netting within 15 feet of the animals and calmly return the way they'd come.

THE LAND ALONG THE SHORE SEEMS TO GET DRIER, MORE FORBIDDING. Trees have all but vanished, and only the occasional scraggly bush dots the horizon. Still, given the starkness of this country, the people live in increasingly refined adobe dwellings that show a level of artistic achievement I haven't yet seen along the Niger: doorways and window frames ornately carved, the mosques with decorated walls and sharply angled minarets.

As night comes, I pull over to a small village of round adobe huts named Nakri. My reception here is unusual compared to what it's been at most other Bozo villages, as the people don't crowd around me and no one asks for money. I think that's half the reason why such enormous crowds have met me at other villages: the people wanted to be nearby should I decide to pass out goodies or spare change. But here in Nakri, a couple of women greet me with the sole intention of finding out what I'm doing on the river. When I ask them if I can spend the night in their village, they enthusiastically say yes.

They lead me to their chief, who's building a canoe nearby. He and the men helping him invite me to look at their work. The canoe is being constructed from a combination of wide slabs of rain forest wood and some remnants from older canoes. The used pieces look in pretty bad shape, have jagged edges and holes, but the men work at joining them to the new pieces of wood as if putting together a puzzle. They fasten the pieces together by heating up and applying a sticky tar, securing them further with wooden pegs. Other men take long planks meant for the hull and curve them in wooden vices laid along the ground. The canoe itself will be a large one when it's finished—maybe 30 feet long and 8 feet across. The process looks laborious, as there's no electricity, no professional tools to help with the building. The men must do everything by hand.

Their construction method is probably similar to Mungo Park's back in 1805, when he sat in Sansanding trying to create a boat for his Niger journey. In Park's case, though, he only put together a couple of rotten canoes sent to him from Mansong, king of Bambarra. Still, just doing that took him an entire month.

The chief stops his work and leads me up to the village, laying out a mat for me to sit on. His wives—he has three, as far as I can tell—offer me some rice for dinner. No one has asked for money or cadeaux yet, which is virtually unprecedented. I can only conclude that the people have never had any tourists visiting their village before, and so they've never had any reason to associate white people with money. And they probably don't have a TV man coming here, either, bringing images of posh Bamako hotels and pampered white guests enjoying cocktails.

The issue of money creates a quandary for me. I want to be generous, paying the women and the chief's family for allowing me to stay and eat with them. People in Mali make on average about ten dollars a week, if that much (for many, it's barely *half* that), so I always try to pay the families I stay with the equivalent of a couple of weeks' wages. In particular, I slip something to the wives and other women, who have less of a chance to make their own money. At the same time, though, I don't want to change forever Nakri village's image of white visitors by passing out bills in front of everyone. So I decide to be secretive about it. I go to where the chief has started working on his boat, and I slip him some money as a gift.

Giving money to the wives, though, proves to be my downfall. I follow them to their cooking area and surreptitiously pass them something, but an old woman catches sight of the bills exchanging hands and all hell breaks loose. Within half an hour, the female populations of both Nakri and the nearby, much larger village of Tindirma have started congregating around me, asking for money. Tindirma, it turns out, borders a dirt road that leads to Timbuktu, and so the people there are especially familiar with white tourists and government workers going by in slick new Land Rovers. Some of them know a little French, and they offer me reasons why they need the money. Sick children, injury, illness. Some of them actually produce children with ailments, but it's not possible for me to help everyone, and I don't want to further damage matters by indiscriminately handing out cash. As for the sicknesses, I probably have the antibiotics that would cure some of the ailments, but, lacking proper medical knowledge, I don't want to play doctor with people's lives.

I do have some bottles of ibuprofen that I brought to Mali to pass out as gifts, and when a couple of old women with painful arthritis come forward I ask a young woman who speaks really good French to translate my instructions for taking the pills. When I hand the bottles over, the old women are so happy to receive them that they hold their hands toward me and start crying. I look down, feeling completely ashamed. Ashamed for all I have, and for all they don't. Ashamed that while American babies live, theirs must die. Mali has one of the highest infant mortality rates in the world: 12 of every 100 babies die. And what to do about any of it? I know that the economy of my own country often flourishes by exploiting other countries' poverty and suffering. Sitting here in Nakri, in front of all these people, I feel a certain culpability from simply being American.

The crowd finally disperses, everyone going home, and peaceful Nakri returns to normal. I walk down to the Niger, just as the setting sun is streaking it with orange light. A storm is coming from the southeast, but I know it will take an hour or so to get here. For now, I study the waters, sighing, thinking about the crowd of women who had surrounded me. I hear a voice and turn to see a woman holding a sick little boy. I recognize her from before; from the descriptions she gave, her child probably has dysentery or giardia: life-threatening ailments without antibiotics.

"Please, madame," she whispers in French, holding out her hand. *"Argent."*

I place some bills in her hand. It is all I can do.

⤳

I WAKE UP IN NAKRI TO THE ROOSTER CALLS, DAY ONLY A GRAY suggestion to the east. My stomach lurches, my guts feeling as if they're being stripped from me. I barely make it out of my tent and through the village to the Niger, where I keep vomiting up bile. Everything in my body feels as though it's turned to liquid. I'm so faint that it's hard to stand, so I kneel and hold my head. Only two days to my goal, and now this.

Some kind of dysentery, probably, though I can't say which one—amoebic, bacillary? I'm hoping it's the latter, which is easier to cure. Still, when I return to my tent to take antibiotics, I immediately throw them up. A group of village folk have risen, and they watch me and tsk. Poor, sick white woman. The children stare, silent and uncomprehending. All I can think about is getting to my goal, reaching my goal, where I can finally stop and lie down, and not have to do anything anymore.

I wash off my face, smooth down my T-shirt. I'm getting to Timbuktu if I have to crawl. The women are still tsking as I take down my tent and load up my kayak. They insist that I stay, but the journey calls. I've come too far to fail now. Hunched over, I get in my kayak and wave goodbye, paddling off toward the morning sun nudging its way through the clouds.

I travel slowly through the intense, rising heat. When I feel too faint, I stop for a while, letting the current take me. But it's a sluggish current, and virtually no help. I try taking some more antibiotics, knowing they would help cure me if I could keep the pills down, but I quickly throw them up. That's the way it goes: vomit, paddle, vomit, paddle. There's been no food in my stomach since the previous evening, but I don't try to eat anything. My appetite is gone, replaced by the painful spasms in my gut and a headache that registers in red spots of faintness before my eyes. Timbuktu feels farther than it ever did. Two days might be two centuries away.

And this is the hottest, most forbidding stretch of the Niger to date, great white dunes swelling on either side of the river, pulsing with heat waves. The sun burns in a cloudless sky that offers up not even a hint of breeze. Strangely, the shores here are more populated than ever, desolate adobe huts regularly breaking the monotony of the desert. The lucky village has a single scraggly tree to provide shade, its branches hanging despondently. I use these tiny settlements as my guideposts, reaching and passing one and then the next, amazed by the Niger's tenacity as it cuts through the Sahara, a gloriously stubborn and incongruous river.

I wonder what Park felt on this stretch. We can never know for sure, having no written record and only unreliable hearsay from his guide, Amadi Fatouma, the sole survivor of the expedition, who claimed that Park and his men had to shoot their way through these waters. Everyone, apparently, wanted Park dead out here.

Which might explain why I'm assailed with angry shouts at every turn, entire villages gathering onshore to yell at me, so that I stick to the very middle of the Niger and carry my can of mace in my lap, paddling as hard as I'm able. Gone are the waves of greeting and friendship from local tribes that I'd experienced at the beginning of my trip. Inexplicably, the entire tone of this country has changed. When I wave hello to people out here, they invariably gesture for me to come and give them money. Add to this the dysentery, which makes me so ill that I frequently have to go ashore, and I spend a great deal of time worrying about where I can stop, and whether, while in the middle of being sick and unable to defend myself, someone might try to rob or hurt me.

Meanwhile, my map becomes even more worthless. None of the turns is where it says it's supposed to be. Short-looking stretches go on interminably. My muscles ache from the dysentery, and my thermometer reads 110 degrees. This is a kind of heat that I've never experienced before, not even when I lived in Tucson for grad school. This heat dissolves into my skin, burns through even the strongest sunscreen, enervates and debilitates. I throw my paddle down, splashing myself with water in an attempt to cool off, though I know by now that it won't work. There is nothing to be done.

There is a certain moment when all resolve goes, when even the most determined person faces the knowledge that they've done the most they can do and the only choice left is to give up. I don't want to admit that I may be at that point, but it sure feels that way. Faint and dizzy, I hold my head down before the midday sun, trying to resist the urge to throw up.

Angry men are shouting at me from a nearby shore, demanding I give them money or cadeaux. When I glance at them, they wave wildly and stamp their feet. I speak to them in English, though I know they can't understand. I ask them if they've seen any good movies lately. I say hello and inquire after their families. I whistle and make strange, enigmatic signs in the air.

The men stop yelling and study me as I float by. It occurs to me that I'm acting like a crazy woman. Which isn't so bad. I actually kind of like it. Not caring anymore.

"Hey, Mungo Park—can you hear me?" I ask the river. "Hey, Mungo—help me out here." I wipe a film of sweat from my face.

Silence. The river's current is so slow that algae grows on the surface of the water.

"Hey, Mun-go!"

I pick up the paddle and start moving again. I pretend it's Mungo Park assisting me, his spirit arriving deus ex machina–style to get me to Timbuktu.

❧

BELOW A LARGE ORANGE DUNE, I SEE THE LONG, RECTANGULAR SHAPE of one of the enormous river barges that ply the Niger. Usually they hold about 60 people plus baggage, are so overloaded that the gunwales barely rise above the water. In this case, though, the boat is nearly empty: must be Rémi's boat. I never know when I'll run into him, was certain he'd be at Timbuktu by now, taking in some air-conditioning and waiting for me to eventually get there. This unexpected meeting is a blessing: not only are they great for mooching, but their boat's canopy is the only shade to be found anywhere on the Niger. I feel as if I could pass out from the sun. Red dots of dizziness have been filling my eyes, regardless of all the water I drink. I could use a secure place to rest for a while.

Rémi waves at me in greeting, and I pull alongside their boat. Heather is reading a copy of the *New Yorker*—for the third time, she tells me—her legs propped up on the table. Rémi attends to his cameras. Behind them, their cook prepares lunch. Will it be boiled chicken with tomato herb sauce and noodles today? Or just fried river fish with French fries? I'm wondering what gave me the dysentery. The rice gruel I had the previous night? Or the rotting fish head at Berakousi?

"How are you doing?" Heather asks me.

"Other than throwing up at a village this morning, I'm fine."

"You catch something?"

"A little dysentery."

"Well," she says, "if it's any consolation, you don't *look* sick."

Which I suppose I don't. I try to keep these matters to myself, usually. And I'll reach a certain point—which I reached long back—where discomfort becomes the norm. All the heat, the sweating, the aching of my body, the dysentery—all of it, normal. So that any luxury, like the bottled mineral water Heather is giving me from their personal stash on the boat, becomes an incredible novelty. I reach deep in my backpack and give her a damp, wadded bundle of pages in return: an issue of *Harper's*.

"Maybe you can dry it out and unstick the pages," I say.

With the shade of their boat's canopy over me, and a bench to rest on, I swallow some antibiotics again and lie down with my hat over my face, knees pulled in against me to try to counter the stomach cramps. Doesn't work. I feel hopelessly nauseous. I hear Heather's comment, *You don't* look *sick,* as I get up, almost mechanically this time, and lower myself into the river to go onshore to throw up. Before I know it, I'm collapsing into the water.

I wake up half in the water, half on shore, retching into the sand. My only hope is that Rémi isn't taking pictures of this. I glance back at the boat to check. Heather is politely feigning an interest in her *New Yorker*. Rémi still seems to be fiddling with his cameras. The three Malian crewmen look out at me, shocked, unsure what to do.

I just lie by myself onshore, retching for a while, unable to get up. The sun is like a glaring heat lamp, weighing me down. It occurs to me that I might call to the others for assistance, but this seems strangely impossible to me. I feel a universe away from them, as if we inhabit different planets; my voice could never possibly travel the light-years' distance. One part of me is fascinated by the fact that I seem absolutely incapable of asking for help. But this is in keeping with my personality. Not to mention that I *chose* this hell, I actually asked for it, and so now I must bask in it—alone.

I slowly get up and trudge off behind a nearby dune. It's strange to no longer see the waters of the Niger before me. This country is all sand and scrub brush. A wasteland. I sit down and stare off at the Sahara. I know it goes on and on for many hundreds of miles. Just the endless sand. To leave the Niger would be to die.

Why did I come here again?

My stomach calms itself and my faintness subsides to a gentle clarity: the post-vomiting high. I look without looking. Like seeing through a window, but no one doing the seeing. Sand dunes flowing toward the horizon. A few bushes. Birds wheeling in the sky.

I know I have two choices: keep going or quit. It's really that simple. But I've come too far now. My goal is too close. All I want to do is paddle again, and keep paddling until this elusive place called Timbuktu is reached, or until I'm unable to go on.

I walk back to the Niger, wading through its waters and getting into my kayak. Rémi hesitates, then says, "I'm not a doctor, but maybe it is good to think about this paddling. Your health is important. You don't have to continue if you're sick."

"I've got to paddle or I'll never reach Timbuktu," I say. I dip my hat in the water and put it on my head.

"I don't want to tell you what to do. I'm not a doctor, but here is my boat. You know what I'm saying?"

I nod. He is offering me the chance to quit, to be taken to Timbuktu in his boat. No one would probably ever know.

"I'm going to paddle," I say.

He holds up his hands. "Okay."

Heather comes over to the side of the boat. "Kira," she says, "just remember that we're here for you."

"Thank you," I say, humbled, and I paddle off into the midday heat.

CHAPTER THIRTEEN

❦

ONE MORE DAY—I HOPE. IF I CAN PADDLE ABOUT 35 MILES TODAY, I can get to Timbuktu by night, but that's quite a distance in a river so sluggish, with my body so weak. I camped in the dunes, awake most of the night from the discomfort in my guts, but I managed to keep down some antibiotics so that I feel stronger now. Or at least as strong as I'll ever get, given the circumstances.

I start early, at first light. I don't have any food left, so I don't eat. Even at eight in the morning, my thermometer reads over 100 degrees, great dunes meeting the river on either side, little adobe villages half-buried beneath them. It is the land of the Tuareg and Moor now, fierce nomadic peoples who crouch down close to shore and stare out at me from their indigo wrappings, none of them returning my friendly waves. Park admitted fearing these people most, as he had been a prisoner of the Moors on his first journey and brutally treated, nightmares of the event plaguing him long after he managed to run away from his captors and return to England. It does not escape my attention that the Tuaregs boast a long history of killing nearly every European traveler who ever tried to reach Timbuktu, including the first woman to make the attempt in 1869. Only by learning to speak Arabic and disguising oneself as a Moor, did the Western traveler have a chance of making it to the fabled city alive. In later years, when France claimed Mali as part of its overseas empire, the colonial government waged nearly nonstop battles against the Tuaregs, but with only limited and short-lived success. They remain an indomitable people, never subjugated, never conquered.

I can imagine Park's trepidation on this part of the journey, in particular, as an island splits the Niger, creating a narrow channel on either side. The narrower the river, the more vulnerable you are. Village people are closer to you, can reach you more easily. There is less opportunity for escape. And this is the most populated stretch of the river to date, sizable villages dotting the shore wherever I look so that I can't evade detection. All I can do is paddle as hard as I can, the people on shore screaming and scolding me as I pass. Crazy people now, people so determined to catch me that they swim into the river after me. I have no way of knowing exactly what their intentions are, though I can tell they're not good, so I follow my new guideline, learned from Park: Don't get out of the boat—*for anything.*

When I float along for a moment to drink some water, men on the shore see it as an opportunity and leap into their canoes, chasing after me and demanding money. I keep my can of mace in my lap and paddle like a madwoman, managing to outrun them. One man comes close enough to hit my kayak with the front of his canoe, nearly grabbing my lead rope with his hand. I'm able to see his face and his wild eyes as I strain to get away. I know one of us will have to give up—him or me. I pace my strokes as if it were a long-distance race, and he stays on my tail for several minutes before falling behind. Swearing at me, he returns to his village.

But it is more of the same at the next village, and at the next after that, so that the mere sight of the pointy canoes on the shores frightens me. No time to drink now, or to splash myself with water to try to cool off. To stop is to give them an incentive to come after me. I round the great bend of the Niger, the sun getting hotter and hotter, my head aching.

The river widens, and I don't see any villages on this stretch. I stop paddling and float in the very middle of the river, nauseous again, and faint, my thermometer reading 112 degrees. I squint at the Niger trailing off into distant heat waves, looking as if it's being swallowed by the Sahara. When Park once asked a local man where the Niger went, he'd replied: "It runs to the world's end." Yes.

"This river will never end," I say out loud, over and over again, like a mantra. My map shows an obvious change to the northeast, but that turn hasn't come for hours, may never come at all. To be so close to Timbuktu, and yet so immeasurably far away. All I know is that I must keep paddling. I *have* to be close. Determined still to get to Timbuktu's port of Korioumé by nightfall, I shed the protection of my long-sleeved shirt, pull the kayak's thigh straps in tight, and prepare for the hardest bout of paddling yet.

I paddle like a person possessed. I paddle the hours away, the sun falling aside to the west but still keeping its heat on me. I keep up a cadence in my head, keep my breaths regular and deep, in synch with my arm movements. The shore passes by slowly, but it passes. As the sun gets ominously low, burning a flaming orange, the river turns almost due north and I can see a distant, square-shaped building made of cement: the harbinger of what can only be Korioumé. Hardly a tower of gold, hardly an El Dorado, but I'll take it. I paddle straight toward it, ignoring the pains in my body, my raging headache. *Timbuktu, Timbuktu!* Bozo fishermen ply the river out here, and they stare at me as I pass. They don't ask for money or cadeaux—can they see the determination in my face, sense my fatigue? All they say is, "*Ça va, madame?*" with obvious concern. One man actually stands and raises his hands in a cheer, urging me on. I take his kindness with me into the final stretch, rounding the river's sharp curve to the port of Korioumé.

I see Rémi's boat up ahead; he waits for me by the port, telephoto lens in hand. It's the first time during this trip that I'm not fazed by being photographed. I barely notice him. I barely notice anything except the port ahead of me. All I can think about is stopping. Here is the ending I've promised myself for weeks. Here I am, 600 miles of river covered, with the port of Timbuktu straight ahead.

Something tugs at my kayak. I'm yanked back: fishnets, caught in my rudder. To be this close, within sight of my goal, and thwarted by yet one more thing. The universe surely has a sense of humor. I jump into the water, fumbling at the nylon netting tangled around the screws holding the rudder to the inflatable rubber. It's shallow here, and my bare feet sink into river mud full of sharp pieces of rock that cut instantly into my soles. I try to ignore the pain, working fast, pulling the netting off until I free my kayak. When I get inside, the blood from my feet mixes with gray river water like a final offering to the Niger. I maneuver around the nets, adjust my course for the dock of Korioumé, and paddle hard.

Just as the last rays of the sun color the Niger, I pull up beside a great white river steamer, named, appropriately, the *Tombouctou*. Rémi's boat is directly behind me, the flash from his camera lighting up the throng of people gathering on shore. There is no more paddling to be done. I've made it. I can stop now. I stare up at the familiar crowd waiting in the darkness. West African pop music blares from a party on the *Tombouctou*.

Slowly, I undo my thigh straps and get out of my kayak, hauling it from the river and dropping it onshore for the last time. A huge crowd has gathered around me, children squeezing in to stroke my kayak. People ask where I have come from and I tell them, "Old Ségou." They can't seem to believe it.

"Ségou?" one man asks. He points down the Niger. His hand waves and curves as he follows the course of the river in his mind.

"*Oui*," I say.

"Ehh!" he exclaims.

"Ségou, Ségou, Ségou?" a woman asks.

I nod. She runs off to tell other people, and I can see passersby rushing over to take a look at me. What does a person look like who has come all the way from Ségou? They stare down at me in my sweat-stained tank top, my clay-smeared skirt, my sandals both held together with plastic ties.

I unload my things to the clamor of their questions, but even speaking seems to pain me now. Such a long time getting here. And was the journey worth it? Or is it blasphemy to ask that now? I can barely walk, have a high fever. I haven't eaten anything for more than a day. How do you know if the journey is worth it? I would give a great deal right now for silence. For stillness.

My exhaustion and sickness begin to alter this arrival, numbing the sense of finish and self-congratulation and replacing it with only the most important of questions. I've found that illness does this to me, quiets the busy thoughts of the mind, gives me a rare clarity that I don't usually have. I see the weeks on the river, the changing tribal groups, the lush shores down by Old Ségou metamorphosing slowly into the treeless, sandy spread near Timbuktu. I'm wishing I could explain it to people—the subtle yet certain way the world has altered over these past few weeks. The inevitability of it. The grace of it. Grace, because in my life back home every day had appeared the same as the one before. Nothing seemed to change; nothing took on new variety. It had felt like a stagnant life.

I know now, with the utter conviction of my heart, that I want to avoid that stagnant life. I want the world to always be offering me the new, the grace of the unfamiliar. Which means—and I pause with the thought—a path that will only lead through my fears. Where there are certainty and guarantees, I will never be able to meet that unknown world.

Night settles on the shore, and Rémi pulls his boat up alongside the cement dock. I deflate my kayak for the last time and pack it up, carrying it and my things onto the boat. Heather and Rémi both give me a hug of congratulation, but I'm still too numb to really comprehend that I've done it yet. To celebrate, Rémi offers me my choice of their onboard selection of soft drinks. I take an Orange Fanta. Outside, barely discernible in the darkness, the crowd of onlookers continues to discuss what I've done. I can hear them exchanging the word "Ségou," and I wonder if they believe that I've paddled this far. But it doesn't matter. I lie down on one of the benches. My head feels hot, and it aches to the metronome-like beating of my heart.

Rémi has gone onshore and tries valiantly to get us a taxi into Timbuktu, but the driver of the only car available at this late hour demands an exorbitant sum of more than $150 to drive 30 kilometers. It is the first time I've seen Rémi get so blustering and assertive, and he argues passionately for a lower sum. We are all hoping for what we've promised ourselves tonight—a hotel room in Timbuktu with blessed air-conditioning—but the driver won't budge his price, thinking he has us. As we're all nearly out of our magazine expense money, I suggest we camp and go to Timbuktu the next morning, when there are sure to be plenty of taxis to take us there at a reasonable price. For the first time, I see this disappointment as just another uncontrollable part of life, like the storms that arose on the Niger. Nothing personal.

I point to the opposite shore as a place to camp away from the crowds. Rémi and Heather agree, and so the great boat is started up and we speed over the Niger beneath a sky dazed with stars. We ground the boat on the opposite shore, and I go about setting up my tent. I'm too sick to fully acknowledge the end of my trip. Rémi offers me a beer to celebrate, but I know I wouldn't be able to keep it down. I do manage to swallow some antibiotics and antinausea pills, which quiet my stomach enough to allow me to eat a mango and some of the noodles Rémi's cook has made for us. As I sit to eat, I'm swaying back and forth in my mind, as if I were still careering over the waves of the Niger. I've heard that this happens to sailors, that they get so attached to being tossed by the waves that they have trouble readjusting to solid ground. For me, it is as if the Niger still keeps a part of me, as if to tell me that I finally belong to it.

Before bed, I sit outside my tent and stare up at the stars.

"Mungo…" I whisper, the Niger licking the muddy shore in the moonlight.

By the dim light from my flashlight, I read the last two letters Park ever wrote, right before he left Sansanding in 1805 to head down the Niger, never to return. The first was to his sponsor, Lord Camden, in which he declared, "I shall set sail to the east with the fixed resolution to discover the termination of the Niger or perish in the attempt … and though I were myself half dead, I would still persevere; and if I could not succeed in the object of my journey, I would at least die on the Niger."

The last letter, different in tone, was to his wife, Ailie:

> *I am afraid that, impressed with a woman's fears and*
> *the anxieties of a wife, you may be led to consider my*
> *situation a great deal worse than it really is. It is true*
> *my dear friends Mr. Anderson [Ailie's brother] and*
> *George Scott have both bid adieu to the things of this*

world; and the greater part of the soldiers have died on the march ... but I still have sufficient force to protect me from any insult in sailing down the river to the sea. We have already embarked all our things, and shall sail the moment I have finished this letter. I do not intend to stop or land anywhere until I reach the coast.... We shall then embark in the first vessel for England.... I think it not unlikely but I shall be in England before you receive this.

I don't think Park believed he would really reach some kind of "coast" and return to England again. His letter to Lord Camden, though resolute and brave, seemed to suggest a kind of futile determination. The Niger's termination was still a mystery to him; he couldn't have known where the river would take him or where he would end up. But what he could be certain of was the heat, the hostility, the myriad dangers at every turn. I think he realized, on some gut level, that those two letters would be the last he would ever write.

And so Park left on his final journey. When he didn't return to England in what was considered a reasonable length of time, the colonial governor of Senegal sent Park's trusty servant Isaaco into the interior in search of him. Years would pass. Then, in 1810, Isaaco reappeared in Senegal with news that Park was dead. What we know of Park's last days comes from the written testimony that Isaaco had collected from Amadi Fatouma, Park's guide during the ill-fated river journey. According to Fatouma, Park had reached Timbuktu's port, where locals started a bloody skirmish: "On passing Timbuctoo we were again attacked by three canoes, which we beat off.... We were reduced to eight hands; having each of us fifteen muskets, always in order and ready for action."

According to another account told to the German explorer Heinrich Barth, who visited Timbuktu years later, Park had actually landed near the city and made contact with the locals, only to be chased away by Tuaregs. And in a final account brought back by the British explorer Hugh Clapperton, Park had made it to his Golden City and was received warmly by the prince. Regardless, he ended up dying on the Niger as he had prophesied, getting as far as Bussa, in modern-day Nigeria, before he disappeared in the river. Drowned? Killed by natives? We'll never know. The Lander brothers, British explorers who visited Bussa in 1830 in an attempt to learn of Park's fate, recovered only his hymnbook and a nautical almanac. Inside the almanac they found some of Park's old papers—a tailor's bill and an invitation dated 9 November 1804, that read, "Mr. and Mrs. Watson would like to have the pleasure of Mr. Park's company at dinner on Tuesday next, at half-past five o'clock. An answer is requested." The great Mungo Park, survived by a dinner invitation.

I catch myself smiling. In the end, I suppose it doesn't really matter what happened to Park. For him, as for me, the journey must be enough.

CHAPTER FOURTEEN

TIMBUKTU.

It is the world's greatest anticlimax. Hard to believe that this spread of uninspiring adobe houses, this slipshod latticework of garbage-strewn streets and crumbling dwellings was once the height of worldly sophistication and knowledge. The "gateway to the Sahara," the "pearl of the desert," the "African El Dorado" is nothing now but a haggard outpost in a plain of scrub brush and sand. After having had such a long and difficult journey to get here, I feel as if I'm the butt of a great joke.

I must content myself with simple rewards. The cold bottle of Coca-Cola I buy from a street vendor. The mango—a mango!—I purchase for the equivalent of 20 cents. Shade trees under which I can stand out of the sun. Shade, a blessing to me now. Such simple things. I stand under the awning of a shop and etch a trail through the dusty clay with the toe of my sandal, the sun like an officious presence, burnishing my skin with heat. I came to terms with it a couple of weeks ago, paddling into the Sahara, our relations cordial now.

The people of Timbuktu stare at me in my T-shirt and skirt, many of them covered as if for a snowstorm, encircled from head to foot in long black chador or indigo wrappings. I wander along a labyrinth of streets, nodding and smiling at them from behind my sunglasses. I'm looking for some vestige of what the explorers of old had promised me I'd find in Timbuktu. Here is the "great object" of Mungo Park's search; in his narrative, he'd described what he'd heard about it: "The present King of Tombuctoo is named *Abu Abrahima;* he is reported to possess immense riches. His wives and concubines are said to be clothed in silk, and the chief officers of state live in considerable splendour." I walk past the baking adobe buildings, taking care to skirt piles of refuse, dung, and rotting kitchen scraps tossed beside the streets. How did everyone get it so wrong?

When Park wrote of this place, the city's true heyday was long expired. Generations of Europeans never knew that a blue-eyed eunuch from the Moroccan court, a Spanish Moor named Judar, had led a Moroccan mercenary army to Timbuktu in 1591 and sacked it. From that point on, Timbuktu would never be the same. Its riches were seized. Its great institutes of scholarship all but vanished. What remained of its former greatness was little more than its name, coined after a woman slave. But "Timbuktu" hasn't lost its power and charm, still inspiring countless people to visit.

During the 14th century, this city had been the domain of one of Timbuktu's most famous patriarchs: Mansa Musa, the emperor of Mali, who amassed huge wealth from the sale of gold, salt, and slaves. He actively sought the conversion of all his subjects to Islam, succeeding in 1336. (The conversion still holds solid, Timbuktu remaining a devoutly Muslim city; its one Protestant mission, around for nearly two decades, reportedly hasn't claimed any converts.) Musa himself made his renowned 6,000-mile pilgrimage across the Sahara to Mecca in 1324, accompanied by 60,000 escorts and 100 camels carrying 300 pounds of gold each. As he passed through Egypt, he gave away so much gold that he caused the metal to depreciate in value for the next ten years. When Musa returned to Timbuktu, he built its most impressive edifice yet, the Great Mosque.

Musa's death led to a period of decline for Timbuktu, marauders and Tuaregs taking turns sacking the city. Ali the Great, ruler of the Songhai empire, finally seized control in 1468; he promptly executed thousands of local leaders but also ushered in a great cultural renaissance that would later inspire the European imagination with tales of an "African El Dorado" deep in the Sahara.

It could be argued that the person most responsible for establishing the myth of Timbuktu in the West was Leo Africanus, the Moor who wrote about his experiences in the city in the early 1500s. Exiled from Spain and then captured by Christian pirates, Africanus was freed by the Medici pope Leo X, and taught Italian. His book *History and Description of Africa and the Notable Things Contained Therein* was published in Italy in 1526. It was translated into English in 1600 and became a popular authority on the mysteries of the desert kingdom. Leo wrote dazzling accounts of Timbuktu:

> There is a most stately temple to be seen … and a princely palace…. Here are many shops of artificers, and merchants, and especially of such as weave linen and cotton cloth. And hither do the Barbary merchants bring cloth of Europe. The inhabitants, and especially strangers there residing, are exceedingly rich, insomuch that the king that now is, married both his daughters unto two rich merchants.
>
> The rich king of Tombuto, hath many plates and sceptres of gold, some whereof weigh 1300 pounds. And

he keeps a magnificent and well-furnished court.…
[H]ere are a great store of doctors, judges, priests, and
other learned men, that are bountifully maintained at
the king's expense.

And hither are brought diverse manuscripts or
written books out of Barbarie, which are sold for
more money than any other merchandise. The coin of
Tombuto is of gold without any stamp or super-
scription; but in matters of small value they use certain shells brought hither out of the kingdom of
Persia.… [T]he inhabitants are people of a gentle and
cheerful disposition, and spend a great part of the night
in singing and dancing through the streets of the city;
they keep a great store of men and women slaves.

Understandably, European governments with colonial aspirations
were eager to see if this account was true. Little matter that Africanus
also described "cottages built of chalk and covered with thatch," or that
he incorrectly described the Niger as flowing westward. The legend was
born. Westerners scrambled to be the first to reach the fabled city. The
Englishman Gordon Laing chose to get there by crossing the Sahara.
He traveled undisguised and with only a local guide, leading many
modern historians to believe that he was out-and-out suicidal.
Miraculously, he reached Timbuktu in 1826—the first European to have
actually entered the city—but he paid a heavy price for the honor: just
before he reached his goal, Tuaregs attacked him. They riddled his body
with gunshot wounds and sword slashes, cutting off his ear, breaking
his jaw, and nearly severing his right hand. Laing spent weeks in a mud
hut in Timbuktu, recovering, only to be strangled to death by Tuaregs
when he attempted to return to Europe across the Sahara. Well into

the 20th century, his bones in their lonely, sandy grave outside Timbuktu made for a popular tourist destination.

Timbuktu's golden myth wasn't officially debunked until the Frenchman René Caillié disguised himself as a Moor, learned Arabic, and crossed the Sahara to reach the city in 1828. History credits him as being the first European to not only get there, but to actually *return* to tell about it—a distinction that was no small feat at the time. He reported what few had suspected: that Timbuktu's wealthy heyday was long over. The German explorer Heinrich Barth was the next to make it to Timbuktu, in 1853. When he finally returned to Europe, he published a book in 1857 that refuted Leo Africanus's lavish descriptions, announcing that the Golden City was "sand and rubbish heaped all round." Others would try to follow him to see for themselves. In 1869 an intrepid 33-year-old Dutchwoman wanted to be the first European woman to get there, but Tuaregs killed her before she made it. Finally, the French military moved in, taking steamers up the Niger, battling local tribes, and raising the tricolors over Timbuktu in 1893— less than 100 years after Park had been the first European to have gazed on the city from the Niger. The French fought the Tuareg for years, defeating them in 1902 after a series of bloody desert battles; the Golden City remained in their hands until Mali's independence in 1960.

I walk Timbuktu's dusty streets. It is 115 degrees already and barely noon, so that I bow under the weight of the sun and every action feels unusually ponderous. I pass wasted-looking donkeys scavenging in rubbish heaps, am careful to avoid the streams of fetid wastewater trailing down alleyways. I visit the homes of past explorers, the Gordon Laings and René Cailliés of history who risked their lives to get here. They were just as disappointed at what they found. Caillié would write that the city and its landscape "present the most monotonous and barren scene I have ever beheld." Later, in 1897, the French explorer Felix Dubois expressed his own unbridled disgust: "These ruins, this rubbish, this wreck of a town, is this the secret of Timbuctou the mysterious?" But I like best what Tennyson said, who had tried to imagine the golden city in his poem "Timbuctoo" before any Westerners had gotten there:

> ... *your brilliant towers*
> *Shall ... shrink and shiver into huts,*
> *Black specks amid a waste of dreary sand,*
> *Low-built, mud-wall'd, barbarian settlements.*

The tourists, mostly flown in on package tours, wilt in the sun as they trudge past me through the streets, searching for whatever it is that Timbuktu had promised them. I fear they too have been disappointed, though this end of the world knows enough to sell them air-conditioned rooms at inflated prices and faux Tuareg wear. I'm learning to move just as slowly, so as not to exert myself in the heat, my every step feeling hazardously close to truth. I see that Timbuktu is better off left to name and fancy. It is a place that's not meant to be found.

⤳

I WANDER AROUND TIMBUKTU AFTER DUSK. I'M TOLD THAT THIS IS dangerous, that unsavory elements may be lurking about, but there is nothing else to do other than sit in my hot room back at the hotel, sweating through my clothes, the overhead fan panting out air. I'm still too sick to eat a full meal or drink a beer at the hotel restaurant, though at least my antibiotics have taken control of the illness.

I had promised myself an air-conditioned room at my journey's end, but the day before I arrived a contingent of foreign aid workers invaded Timbuktu in their brand new Land Rovers, seizing all such rooms in town. Rémi is back among them, drinking beers. He spent part of this afternoon trying to secure an air-conditioned room for Heather and himself, bribing and cajoling hotel managers. He failed, and so he has vowed—as I have—to leave this city as soon as possible. He said he has never, on any of his prior travels, experienced a heat as bad as Timbuktu's. I would have to agree. Strangely, the night offers no respite from the hot temperature, and only the occasional whiff of a breeze gives faint relief. At any rate, it is better to remain outside at all costs.

The stifling heat lasts well into night. I make my way past the empty market, walking between adobe houses. I casually look around for *antars*—genies. Most of the people in Timbuktu believe in these spirits. There are black and white ones, the whites considered more powerful. They show themselves in a number of different ways. Most often, they appear as a black spot on the ground ahead of you, which expands into enormous size if you stare at it. They also come in the form of stray dogs or cats, which vanish as soon as you go near them. Some genies take the appearance of short, squat, black-skinned men with long beards and feet that point backward, which cause mischief in people's houses.

Walking outside at night, as I am, is supposed to be the best way to come in contact with them. During a full moon, genies will throw stones at you. They can also smell a man who has just had sex with a woman, and they will beat him as he walks home. Cat genies speak your name as you pass by, and if you turn to answer them, they'll show you something so terrible that you'll go crazy. People regularly go crazy from genies (I'm told). They also fight with genies, die from genies. Genies have been known to kidnap people and cause them to disappear in the desert. Especially evil genies enjoy filling the streets of Timbuktu with vagrants and insane people. Witches are the only ones who willingly cavort with the genies of Timbuktu, performing secret *holo-hori* dances, during which they summon the genies to a spot in the desert and become possessed by them. Then they will dance so crazily that they'll actually die if people don't severely beat them with sticks to make the genies leave their bodies.

I look for dark spots on the ground ahead of me, but see nothing. Timbuktu keeps its secrets. Only a stray cat walks by, forgetting to call out my name.

⌒

I DON'T WANT TO LEAVE MALI WITHOUT TRYING TO FREE A COUPLE OF slaves, an objective I've had since the beginning of my trip. I carry a couple of large gold coins from home, thinking that if I'm able to free anyone, they can start a business for themselves with the money.

It's not an easy thing to free slaves in a country where slavery is technically illegal, and where the government will readily insist that no such thing exists. But it does. There is an entire underclass in Mali known as the Bella people, a race of West Africans who have been the traditional slaves of the Moors and the Tuaregs—Arab peoples—for centuries. It is a classic and tragic lesson in human irrationality. Mali's Tuareg, with their olive complexions and light-colored hair and eyes, believe themselves to be a Caucasian people, and therefore distinct from the Bella, who are darker-skinned and have physical features associated with sub-Saharan Africans. The Tuareg can thus claim a superiority over the Bella, which helps justify the oppression of them.

This prejudice extends to Malian culture at large, where a Bella is thought to be stupid, ugly, poor, worthless. One does not eat with a Bella, not even in the worldly towns of Mopti and Bamako. To call someone a "Bella" is a grave insult, a way to pick a fight. The rare Bella who does manage to make something of himself will usually tell everyone that he's a Songhai, being completely shamed into denying his heritage. Or, if he has the courage not to hide who he is, he faces the jealousy and wrath of other Malians, who believe that the Bella, as eternal slaves, don't deserve any success.

I have been increasingly dismayed by what I've learned about the situation of the Bella in Mali, which is why I'd like to help someone if I can. In Timbuktu, I go in search of them, and find them living in haggard huts near the garbage dumps. Most of these people work for the Tuareg in one capacity or another. The women do all a Tuareg family's domestic duties, from the cooking, washing, and cleaning, to hairdressing; Tuareg males will also force them into sexual acts. The male Bella acts as a Tuareg man's personal servant, or he is a shepherd or farmer. Occasionally, the Tuareg master will offer the services of his Bella to others, getting any monies received. Most Bella who are still slaves are not allowed to keep their own wages and must rely on their masters for all things in life.

I've contacted Assou, sending him a round-trip bus fare to come up from Mopti. I'm thinking he can help me look into the possibility of freeing a slave or two, as he grew up in Timbuktu and knows the right people. Assou has refused to accept any money for his assistance, wanting to free the women as badly as I do. He is fond of saying to me that "what you do for others, you do for yourself." His eyes get moist when he speaks of the Bella. Back in Mopti, he told me a secret: that he considers himself one of them. Though he's Songhai by birth, he was breastfed by his mother's Bella friend, which by Malian standards makes him part-Bella. "The Bella are in my blood," he told me. It was a daring admission for him to make, and I had to swear not to reveal his story to any Malians as he thought it could hurt his career. But he said that his parents had always stood up for people like the Bella. They always treated everybody the same. And he had learned from them.

I meet Assou at my hotel, and I ask him if we can go together to visit a Tuareg family. I want to see how they interact with their Bella servants. The family we visit lives in an adobe hut on the outskirts of Timbuktu. I greet three corpulent women who are spread out on mats under a thatch awning. They have light complexions and straight black hair, looking not unlike women from India. They wear large gold earrings, and the henna on their hands and feet makes it seem as if they wear maroon-colored gloves and socks.

The head Tuareg woman works with leather, so I ask her if she could put my prayer paper from Big Father into a special leather saphie pouch. She agrees, greeting us cordially and offering us chairs and cups of tea. It is a young Bella woman, however, who brings us these things. The girl is lanky, scrawny, barefooted, her hair in crude cornrows. She wears a ratty pagne and moves with slow deliberation, her eyes making contact only with her feet. She doesn't speak and isn't spoken to except by way of an order.

"Is that girl a Bella slave?" I ask Assou in English, a language the saphie woman can't understand. We watch the girl serving the Tuareg women some tea.

"Yes, of course," he says.

"How do you know?"

"I know this family. They don't pay her money. She belongs to them."

"Couldn't she just leave if she wanted to?"

Assou laughs. "They'd find her and bring her back. She *belongs* to them."

"They'd punish her?"

"Yes. Look," he says, "how they don't feed her anything, but they are all fat. Look."

I glance from the skinny Bella girl to the well-fed Tuareg women. The one who is busy fashioning a piece of leather around my prayer paper suddenly snaps out an order. The Bella girl rushes forward to take away our teacups, and the Tuareg woman glances at us as if to say, *It's hard to find good help these days.* It is my first glimpse of the relationship between these two peoples.

I leave with Assou, my saphie hanging on a string around my neck. I think I can understand why the Bella have remained in a perpetual state of servitude. Their condition goes beyond the fear of a Tuareg master's coming to reclaim them or punish them if they run away, beyond the economic poverty that keeps them reliant on their masters. I see that it stems from an entire frame of mind that batters their self-esteem into submission from the very day of birth. They are not born to their mothers, but rather to the Tuareg family that owns them. I wonder if they believe they could ever have the means to achieve anything better for themselves? It is the consciousness of the downtrodden.

CHAPTER FIFTEEN

∾

HISTORY STILL PERVADES TIMBUKTU, SLAVERY BEING ONE OF THE most secretive and ongoing of all the old institutions. If you mention the idea of slavery in Mali to some experts, though, they'll be quick to cite the 1971 law that supposedly abolished it, insisting that the Bella are now paid workers, having freedom of movement and civil rights. In short, they're not "slaves" anymore. But people living in Timbuktu tell a completely different story: that the Bella are slaves by deed if not by word, are still a form of "property" that the Tuareg refuse to give up, are often raped or beaten by their masters, forced to live on the fringes of society, and to turn over any money they earn. So is it "slavery," then, or is it not? But beyond the semantic debate rests a more fundamental question: Where does all this wordplay leave the Bella at the end of the day?

When researching the slavery situation before my trip, I was perplexed by recent U.S. State Department reports that conclude that de facto slavery still exists in Mali. Why had an entire group of people remained the equivalent of slaves in a country that claims that slavery isn't happening anymore? Was there no recourse for them? Which is when I mulled over the feasibility of actually freeing someone—which isn't without its own degree of controversy. Some people familiar with the region asserted that wasn't possible, that I'd only be duped by those involved in the negotiations. Others argued that, at least on a psychological and economic level, the Bella remain hopelessly tied to their Tuareg masters, so that even if I could free someone, they'd be left without the means to provide for themselves.

Yet, suppose I really *could* free someone? Just suppose. And then, what if I gave someone enough money to start up a business and become self-sufficient? Wouldn't this be preferable to the alternative: dehumanizing, often brutal servitude for the rest of one's life? After studying and debating all the facts, I finally concluded that it was worth a try.

My understanding about the situation in Timbuktu is that it mirrors what's happening a bit farther to the north, in Mauritania, where the slavery issue is well publicized and is starting to be addressed by aid organizations and the government alike. Mali, however, seems to be in a state of denial. I've learned that some of the Tuareg living in the Timbuktu area would release their Bella from servitude if someone would simply compensate them for officially letting them go. Before the 1971 law was passed, the Tuareg could sell their Bella, contract them out, or put them to work for the master's family, keeping all monies the individuals made, so that the idea of simply "giving these people away" because of a decree made in distant Bamako seemed akin to tossing away valuable merchandise for no good reason. After all, what do those rich men in the government know? Many Tuareg flat-out refused, and though they'll claim their Bella are free to come and go as they please, it is just a means of subterfuge—they have to say that. (Just as people have spun me the official line: "There is no female genital mutilation in Mali; it's against the law"—when organizations like

Amnesty International and the World Health Organization have esti-mated that at least 90 percent of Malian women still undergo the pro-cedure.) And with no one in the Malian government willing to investigate the matter, and no authorities willing to charge people with the crime, the tacit slavery flourishes as if no law had been enacted at all.

This isn't to say that some Bella didn't take charge and leave their former masters after the emancipation law was passed—many did. I found some of them living on the outskirts of Mopti or Bamako, in squalid thatch huts, on worthless plots of land, or on the edge of city garbage dumps. Suddenly becoming free without sufficient funds to start life anew meant that even those Bella who managed to obtain a guarantee of emancipation were forced to live in the same villages where they had been kept in servitude, psychologically and economically dependent on their former masters as if they were still enslaved. All of this emphasizes that freedom is worthwhile only if Bella have the means of starting businesses *independent* of their former masters, which is what I want to arrange if I can actually free someone.

To that end, Assou has been helping me out. His Tuareg friend has been acting as middleman, speaking to the head of his own and other Tuareg families to see if they could spare a female Bella or two. In addi-tion, Assou has enlisted the help of his "second mother," the Bella woman who had once breastfed him. She is speaking to the elders in various Bella families, trying to identify a couple of young women who might benefit the most from being freed. I've requested that they be women, who face a very real possibility of seeing themselves or their daughters raped.

And now a breakthrough: Assou has found a Tuareg chief willing to sell a Bella or two. Assou and I work to ensure the legitimacy of this arrangement, though everything must be done in secret because "slav-ery doesn't officially exist in Mali." Assou will be the one to pass on the money to the women's Tuareg master, "Zengi" (he didn't want to reveal his real name). He must pretend to be the one in charge of the negotiations, or none of this can happen. He has told Zengi that he's freeing the women as part of his college "research" and that I'm coming along to help him take notes. Also, he needs a couple of photos for his research, and so there will be someone along to take photographs. This is what has been approved by Zengi. Under no circumstances must Assou let on that I'm a writer or that any of this is my idea.

Negotiations settled, Assou and I arrive at the Bella village with Rémi. We sit in the midst of the small thatch huts. The Bella have been told that Assou is arriving today and that their Tuareg master has requested their presence in the village. So they are all sitting here now, staring at us—old and young, children half-clothed, women cradling infants. Assou admits he doesn't know which two women have been chosen to be sold to me, so that I stare back at each of them, trying to know what it is like to be them. To wake up each day knowing you are owned by another, unable to marry without the master's permission, unable to travel without his leave, unable to earn your own money or buy your own shoes. Zengi is sole arbitrator of their lives, and I want to see this man, look into his eyes, know some inkling of what lies in his heart, what drives him.

There is a brief wait, as he lives separately from them, among his own people; the Bella here report to him and his family each day for their work duties. A car arrives and Zengi steps out. He is cloaked in indigo wrappings, the Tuareg man's traditional wear of the desert. I can see only his eyes as he daintily holds the bluish material over his nose and mouth, as if afraid of catching a cold. He sits down on a mat before "his Bella," as he calls them. He coddles one older man, stroking the man's arm and patting him as one might a favorite pet.

I have Assou ask him if these people are his slaves.

"Slavery is illegal in Mali," he says calmly.

"But they are *your* Bella?" I ask.

He nods his head.

Rémi comes forward with his camera to take a picture of him, and Assou angrily waves him back. "Not yet," he says quickly, and glances at Zengi to see if he's on to us: that this event isn't about Assou's "research."

Fortunately, he looks unfazed.

"Are they paid monthly wages?" I ask.

He tells me, through Assou, that he gives them a place to live, stock to raise, the clothes on their back. When one of them gets married, he provides animals for the bride price. This, I'm to understand, is their "pay."

I turn to a middle-aged woman who is sitting nearby. "If she wanted to leave here, go to Mopti and not come back, could she?" I ask him.

Zengi's face-wrapping falls for a moment, revealing a trace of a smirk. "Either I kill her, or she kills me," he says, which is to say, "Over my dead body." He readjusts his face-wrapping again, just his hazel eyes visible.

There are words in the Bella language for the distinctions between master and slave. *Terché* refers to those Tuaregs who have slaves; *aklini* is the actual word for "slave," which is still in everyday use. The fact that they have these words, still *use* these words, speaks to the tacit master-slave arrangement that continues to exist among these peoples.

I ask which women are to be freed and whether the money I passed on to Assou is sufficient for the purchase of one or two people. They talk for a while, and Zengi holds up two fingers. Assou says that he will free two women, household helpers that he has decided he can spare as he has three others already, and sufficient Bella babies to fill future vacancies. Their price is to be considered a bargain and a sign of his beneficence: the equivalent of $260, more than Mali's GDP per household for one year.

He motions to a couple of young women standing at the edge of the crowd. They approach us with apprehension.

"These are the women," Zengi says. He orders them to take a seat on the mat before me. One of them, I notice, holds a sickly looking baby girl.

"She has a baby," I tell Assou. "Ask him if he can include the baby with her mother."

Assou does, and a brief discussion ensues. "He won't," Assou says.

"Then ask him how much the baby is." I can't believe such a sentence has come out of my mouth, but Assou is asking him now and Zengi is sitting up regally, shaking his head.

"He won't sell the baby," Assou says. He leans closer to me. "He's already giving us a favor by selling two people. It's best, when a person gives you a favor, not to ask for more."

Which I take to be a warning. No more will be sold, Assou tells me, because they're too valuable. A little boy nearby, for example, is to be Zengi's son's personal servant. The value of "his Bella" depends not only on age and occupation, but on how closely the Tuareg family relies on their services. In the case of the two women sitting before me, they're fairly dispensable and replaceable, and thus, cheap.

I'm staring at the little girl, wondering what will become of her, but there is nothing to be done. While I know that her mother can still live in this village and won't be physically separated from her child, the girl remains bound to a life of servitude to Zengi's family as soon as she's big enough to work. I already feel that telltale numbness coming over me, that suppression of emotion that I invoke whenever I can't deal with something. Better not to feel anything. So I stand up and tell Assou I'd like to get this over with. Pay Zengi his money. Buy these people already.

Zengi follows us behind a nearby hut—he doesn't want "his Bella" to see him receiving money for their family members (apparently even he is capable of the rare twitch of conscience)—and Assou hands him the money. My personal money, which I never seem to have enough of and which I certainly don't want Zengi to get. But there is no way around it. And the Tuareg man pockets the bundle of bills and leads us back to the crowd of waiting Bella. With a regal wave of his hand, he directs the two women to us.

"Go with them," he tells them. "You belong to them now. I'm finished with you."

And the shocked looks on their faces are hardly what I expected. Hell, I don't know what I expected, but definitely not this. The two women obediently follow us as we walk away from the throng. I have no idea what to say to them, and I ask Assou to tell them that I did this—bought them—so that they'd be free. So that they won't belong to anyone, and can go and get a job if they'd like, earn some wages, live without having to bow down to another.

The women just stand in front of me. One of them, Fadimata, is smiling, but the other, Akina, looks as if someone's just smacked her in the face. I hand them each a gold coin I brought from home for this purpose, worth about $120 apiece, as well as some Malian money. I have Assou tell them that this was all my idea, and that this money is meant to help them start a business, get a footing somehow.

The women nod. Fadimata is thanking me, but Akina holds her head down silently. I don't understand what's wrong, so I ask if we can go somewhere to be alone, away from Zengi, who is standing nearby, mummy-like in his indigo wrappings, explaining the situation to the other Bella. We head into a thatch hut and sit on the sandy floor. The women sneak glances at me, Fadimata holding her—or perhaps I should say Zengi's—baby in her arms. They have hidden the gold coins and money in their palms, and now they really look at them for the first time.

I've never been good at small talk, particularly not with people I've just purchased.

"So will you start a business now?" I have Assou ask them.

Fadimata replies: "I'll try to get some millet or rice to sell in the Timbuktu market." Though she'll probably stick around this village because of her baby, she'll be self-sufficient. Any produce that she sells in the market, any money she makes, is hers now. She won't have to report to Zengi.

"Have you liked working for him?" I ask her.

"No," she says immediately. "I want to live my own life and have my own business."

"What do you think about your baby belonging to him?"

"I have no choice," she says, glancing down at the child and caressing her head.

Akina holds her head down and says nothing. I ask her if she liked working for Zengi's family.

"No," she mumbles, looking at her hands.

"Are they nice to you?" I ask.

She shakes her head, refusing to look at me.

"Do they hurt you?" I ask.

Softly, she says that they beat her. Fadimata nods in affirmation. She says that they beat her too.

I don't know how to ask the next question, but I feel I must. I ask them if any of the Tuareg men have ever taken them ... raped them.

The women are silent.

I have Assou tell them that they're safe talking to me, that I'm not going to tell any of the Tuareg what they say, that I'm their friend.

"It didn't happen to me," Fadimata says. "But it happened to my friend. She told me."

Akina nods in agreement but says nothing. She looks downright scared, and she fingers her dress, frowning.

I have Assou ask her if she's OK. She looks up at me, looks into my eyes for the first time. "I feel shame," she says, "about what happened."

"Shame?" I ask Assou.

And it comes out that she feels ashamed that she was sold like some animal. She feels ashamed to be sitting in front of me.

"No," I say. "Tell her not to." I reach over and take hold of her hand. She stares at me; we've got tears in our eyes. I keep squeezing her hand. "Tell her not to feel ashamed."

Assou tells her, and it is as if a transformation comes over her. Her whole countenance changes, relaxes, and she is able to look into my eyes. When I ask her if she'll tell me how the Tuareg have hurt her, she becomes animated. She stands, and she imitates someone beating another person on the back. Her hands come up and down with an imaginary stick, as if trying to drive it through the body of another. When she stops, the expression on her face is one of pure rage, pure hatred. Both women tell me that they're beaten daily, for no reason whatsoever.

They explain to me that they must do everything for their Tuareg masters, and it is a description I've heard from other Malians—that the Tuareg consider themselves an aristocratic race, above performing everyday tasks. The domestic servants buy food for the family, prepare it, farm the land, cook, pound millet. Basically, they do all the work, so that the family has leisure.

"So if a Tuareg's sitting here and wants a bottle that's out of reach," I say to the women, "do you have to bring it to him?"

They both smile and nod adamantly. "We have to bring everything to them," Fadimata says. She imitates a Tuareg woman holding her hand out. "Like this: take and bring." We all laugh—Akina the loudest. It's nice to see her smiling.

I inquire how old the women are, and their answer surprises me— maybe 18 or 19. They don't know for sure because no birth certificates were drawn up. But they look much older than that; they *feel* much older, as if their unpleasant experiences with Zengi's family have aged them irrevocably.

I ask the women if they can move away now, go to Mopti if they want. I'm wondering what guarantee there is—if any—that they won't be reclaimed the minute I leave.

"No, he can't," Fadimata says. Akina nods in agreement. "We're free now. We have his promise. When he told us to go with you, that meant everything. 'Go,' is a guarantee that means, 'You're free.'"

I can only hope they're right. Still, in a society that refuses to acknowledge the ongoing reality of slavery, there can be no official papers drawn up, no receipts. If Zengi is honorable, upholds his part of the bargain—as the women assure me he will—then they have nothing to worry about. And the fact that they are already planning their futures, telling me about the millet they will buy, is enough to reassure me. For now. At any rate, perhaps they won't be beaten or humiliated anymore.

When I get up to leave, shaking each of their hands, they tell me that God will bless me, will take care of me for what I've done for them. They keep repeating *albaka*—thank you—over and over. I'm grateful to see their happy expressions, though I don't know what to say. Maybe Fadimata can buy her baby if she makes enough money. I don't have words.

⌐◝

I CAN'T SEEM TO FORGET THE TWO WOMEN BACK IN THE BELLA village. All I want to do is leave Timbuktu, go home. But before I do, I ask Assou if he will take me to the Djingarey Berre mosque to see the door that—if opened—will end the world. This mosque is Mali's oldest, built by the great Songhai king Mansa Musa in the 14th century, after his return from Mecca. It has survived the centuries virtually intact and now sits on the edge of town, spiked adobe minarets reaching skyward, garbage swirling about its walls.

We have the mosque to ourselves, the caretaker busy with tourists on the roof. Inside, it is dim and cool. Faint light trails down from skylights, exposing the clouds of dust kicked up by our feet. It is hugely empty here, the adobe walls revealing the pressing of ancient hands.

The special door is in a nondescript wall along the far side of the mosque, hidden behind a simple thatch mat. Assou tells me that no one is shown the real door anymore. He doesn't know why. Perhaps it's too dangerous. He once glimpsed it when he was a boy, but he doesn't remember it.

"I want to see what it looks like," I say.

Assou laughs. "I never met anyone as curious as you."

"I'm serious."

"Then go look." But I notice that he, himself, is scared.

The empty mosque rings with our voices. Dust swirls in the shafts of light. Kittens lie in the shadows of the columns, their ears flickering to the sounds of our voices. There are more kittens here than I've ever seen in one place, their bellies gently rising and falling, their eyes half-closed and Buddha-like.

I creep forward and gently pull back the mat. And here it is: the door that can end the world. It is made exclusively of wood, the middle part rotted away. It looks unremarkable, like a piece of faded driftwood. Suddenly, impulsively, I stick a hand out and touch it.

The world doesn't quake. The waters don't part. The earth continues on its axis, churning out immutable time.

"The world hasn't ended," I declare, my voice echoing along the far walls.

"You must *open* it," Assou says, laughing.

And I could open it, standing here as I am with the caretaker blithely unaware on the roof of the mosque. For an insolent moment I pretend I hold the world in my hands. I think of Zengi and the slave women. I think of the Fulani women teaching me how to cook. I see that Bozo fisherman in his canoe, cheering me on to Timbuktu. It is such a kind yet cruel world. Such a vulnerable world. I'm astounded by it all.

EPILOGUE

⌒

HOMEBOUND, FINALLY. I LEAN BACK IN MY SEAT, MY FLIGHT TO Bamako making a complete mockery of my kayak trip. From this height, all those weeks spent on the river have been reduced to mere seconds as we speed by. I look out of the window. Park's majestic Niger appears as a feeble trail of gray, cutting through desert plains, winding around pale hills, and emerging in an unassuming puddle that is Lake Debo. It took me a day to cross that lake, and another two days to battle around the northern buckle of the Niger that empties from it, those days surrendered now to a shuddering passage at 15,000 feet.

Clouds block out the scene. I turn the air-conditioning knob to full power and shut my eyes, feeling utterly exhausted. Is this what it's like to enter a second birth? But there are no Dogons around to ask. I know only that there's no returning to the way I was before this trip. I finger the seatbelt, slack and useless around me. This is the airline—Air Mali—that the U.S. State Department advised me against using. Well, I've broken my last rule then, but I wouldn't paddle up the Niger if all the geniuses in Washington paid me. There is one thing that Mungo Park never understood and that I finally have: the journey will always tell you when it's over.

ACKNOWLEDGMENTS

∽

THIS TRIP COULD NOT HAVE HAPPENED, NOR THIS BOOK HAVE BEEN published, without the help and generosity of my editor Steve Byers at *National Geographic Adventure*. He sent me on my first assignment, published my first national magazine article, and has offered Byers-size helpings of support and enthusiasm ever since. I wouldn't be where I am right now if it weren't for him. Thank you.

Many thanks to Val Wedel, patient recipient of my forlorn e-mails from unpleasant corners of the world. I don't know what I'd do without your friendship and support.

Huge thanks to Matthew Flickstein, Ginny Morgan, Wiley Miller, Cheryl Graham, Heather Kilpatrick, Trudy Lewis, Miyoko Goto, and the wonderful people in the Show Me Dharma sangha.

Gloria in Excelsis Deo.